GW00949735

BACK YARD

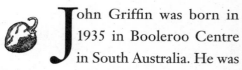

John Griffin was born in 1935 in Booleroo Centre in South Australia. He was a high school teacher for thirty-six years before retiring to his garden. John has written many short stories and had ten radio plays broadcast, as well as publishing two books of poetry. John Griffin believes that going home to a garden eases many of the world's problems.

BACK YARD

A Gardening Life

JOHN GRIFFIN

Wakefield Press

Promotion of this book was assisted
by the South Australian government
through Arts South Australia.

Wakefield Press
Box 2266
Kent Town
South Australia 5071

First published 1997

Copyright © John Griffin, 1997

All rights reserved. This book is copyright.
Apart from any fair dealing for the purposes of private study,
research, criticism or review, as permitted under the Copyright Act,
no part may be reproduced without written permission.
Enquiries should be addressed to the publisher.

Designed by Kerry Argent, Adelaide
Edited by Celia Jellett
Typeset by Clinton Ellicott, MoBros, Adelaide
Printed and bound by Hyde Park Press, Adelaide

National Library of Australia
Cataloging-in-publication entry

Griffin, John, 1935–   .
Back yard.

ISBN 1 86254 393 3.

1. Backyard gardens – Australia. 2. Gardening – Australia.
3. Family recreation – Australia. I. Title.

643.550994

For Giovanni Domenico Gervasi

born 24 October 1900

Contents

Part One

Swings and Things 3
Good with His Hands 10
Carpentry Lesson 14
The Comelli Collection 15
Archaeology of the Suburban Dream 22
Ritual 26
My Father, Visiting 28
Bump in the Night 32
Did You Sleep Well, Dear? 35
Rain in Summer 36
Possum Weather 37

Part Two

Fortress Giovani 45
Catsday 48
Another Learning Experience for Dad 50
Pompey 51
Cat and Commodore 52
Mushrooms 53
For Andrew 56
Willow, Willow 57
Willow 60
Green Lily 61
Mr Belvedere 65
A Tale of Two Bird Baths 68
Mrs Quarter and Me 71
Blue-tongue Lizard 74
My Son and the Lizard 79
The Gecko 80
The Athel Pine at the Desert's Edge 81
Air Raids 85
Schinus Molle and Mud Pies 88
The Bad Plant 90
Pecking Order 93
Cocky 98

Love of Magnolias   99
Olé for Chestnuts   101
Something Nasty from Port Lincoln   105
Lemons and Lots of Sugar   109
Cheap Mulch   112
A Million Ways with Compost   116
The Quail   122
Melancholy Season   126
The Beans   127
Officially Autumn   128
Autumn   129
The Old Tomatoes   130
Cleaning Up   132

Part Three
Nineteen Things I Have
   Learnt About Carrots   135
A Minuet with Lettuce   142
Italian Lettuce   149
Glut of Tomatoes   151
A Rash Thing with Radishes   159
Very Sexy Veg   162
Pollination   169
Coping with Chillies   171
Companion Planting   177
Herb of Grace O'Sundays   183
Tarragon Vinegar   187
Rosemary Remembered   190
Rosemary   193
Tamarillo   194
Plum Sunday   196
Night and Plums   199
The Carthaginian Dwarf   200
Lilly Pilly   205
Yard's End   210
Giant of Stuttgart   211

Part One

Swings and Things

The back yard, and the therapy of gardening, must be the Australian suburb's contribution to sanity. Yet the peasant pottering that I enjoy so much, and the things that go with raising a family in the suburbs, may not be easily understood. Imagine if a mechanical explorer from Mars had settled its tripod legs on someone's lawn late at night, once a year over several years, and beamed back to its vegetable masters a picture of life on this planet, before returning to its orbit. The Martians would have seen an inexplicable series of pseudo-machines standing on the grass.

How could you, in a scientific and rational vegetable world such as Mars might be, where the concept of play is unknown, explain a tiny yellow-and-blue bicycle with trainer wheels attached, left on its side beside a small above-ground pool with a blue liner, half full of water and containing a floating pink duck and a wooden spoon?

The progress of a family with children can be seen in the changing face of the back yard. Ours began, two back yards back in time, with Emma's first small, safe bicycle, and a small pool.

The birth of John meant a move to a larger house, where we lived for two years. Here, the trainer wheels were taken off and Emma was away on the bike around the block by herself. The pool had come with us when we moved to this house, and reflected the sunlight back into space right through each of the summers we were there.

I did the first bricklaying I had ever done, while we lived at this house, to make a small sand pit for Emma and John. It was behind the shed, under the shade of a fifty-year-old grapefruit tree.

At this house the children had their first swing, given to them by Tina's parents for Christmas. It was one of those that could accommodate two children, and it must have clocked up thousands of air miles before it was finally donated, many years later, to the St Vincent de Paul Society. When it squeaked, I had to oil it, and slowly the red paint flaked off it and the rust started.

Then, in 1972, my mother-in-law died suddenly, and my father-in-law Giovanni asked us to move in with him. He would sell us the house and we would build a bedroom and bathroom for him. Giovanni was seventy-two years old, still working, and much loved by the children.

We settled in to a three-generation extended family and moved beyond our grief to a happy accommodation with each other, with Grandpa in his new rooms at the back of the house. Later he moved to the front of the house, when we rearranged the rooms to provide a bedroom for Andrew, our third child.

The swing came with us, but the sand pit couldn't, and

so I bought some perma-pine posts and built another, at the end of the yard by the clothes line. When, years later, Andrew tired of it, there was not a great deal of sand left, and I retired the posts to the piles of junk behind the shed. Occasionally, a dinosaur or a Matchbox car, lost in that long-ago sand pit, surfaces in the soil in that corner of the garden.

We bought an old kindergarten desk for a couple of dollars at a secondhand shop, and Grandpa made small chairs for the children to sit on. These were often taken outside, and left on the lawn instead of being brought inside when darkness came.

John had a huge three-wheeler bicycle, which he rode up and down the street with all his competitive and frantic energy. Then, one afternoon, he left it in the driveway when he came in to the evening meal. It began to rain, and so nobody went outside until next morning. Someone (a Martian perhaps) removed it during the night, and the insurance company agreed to replace it since it had been stolen from the property.

The replacement was rarely used, because in the interim John, a boy of extraordinary determination, took over his sister's bicycle and, a few days before his second birthday, after a number of bloody tumbles and much gravel rash, mastered the skill of riding a two-wheeler. Emma protested the loss of her wheels, and so we bought the next in a long succession of bikes.

When he was about six, John was given a splendid battery-driven blue aeroplane, about 40 centimetres long with a similar wing span. For weeks this plane whizzed and whirred around the playroom floor and on the front verandah, but eventually the mechanism broke down and the plane was abandoned.

But not for long. Grandpa had an idea, and more or less secretly set about bringing it into being. What he created was a great joy to John and Andrew. Our yard slopes slightly from north to south, as it does from east to west, and Grandpa erected some poles and strung a wire from them between the house and the shed; soldered a loop to the top of the plane; devised a spring-loaded contraption at the back of the house; and launched the blue plane, on its guide wire, so that it ran the length of the yard, followed by two very happy boys. They played with it frequently and were the envy of their friends, who all arrived to try it out. Sometimes, when the children were inside, we would hear the plane running on its wire down the yard. It was the inventor, tinkering to adjust it, or sometimes just playing.

At a later stage, when the plane had fallen to pieces, the poles and wire were given another function. The guide wire was extended along the eaves and connected to a handle in Grandpa's room, at one end, and to a jangling set of bird-scaring lids and bells among his fruit trees at the other end. He could sit in his room, watch television, tug the handle, and believe he was keeping the birds away from his figs.

The boys had many Matchbox cars during their early years, and raced them along the paths, on the playroom floor, and in Grandpa's room. So Grandpa put his ingenuity to work again, and built an inclined plane about 2 metres long. This sat at the back of the house (there were rails to stop the cars going over the edge of the runway) and the racing cars got a boost from gravity and streaked down the path further and faster than ever.

Emma had a friend who did gymnastics, and who had a climbing frame at home. Our acquisition stood on the lawn, was moved occasionally, and kept three children amused for many years before it was, in its turn, given away.

I even enjoyed it myself and, sitting on the top rung, could see into all the neighbouring back yards.

Then came the trampoline – a full-sized one. This was a Christmas present – not gift-wrapped, but delivered to the front verandah and left there, with the children believing the story that it was their aunt's present for their family of four cousins who lived a couple of hundred metres away.

The trampoline gave Emma, John and Andrew, and their cousins and friends, endless hours of fun. I looked enviously at them, and then, one late afternoon, when there was no one else around, I climbed on it and began to bounce. I could see over the edge of the world.

I was also the object of much merriment to my neighbour, who was out in the yard and saw my fairly large shape rising above and falling below her horizon. She let me know, with great delight. End of my adventure.

The trampoline was an exciting focus for the boys' parties, but as they grew it fell out of use. I began to notice that it had a new function. Emma would change into her bathers, take a book, and sunbathe on it. John followed the practice, but even this tapered off. When I dismantled it, because it was too large to fit into the van the St Vincent de Paul collectors used, the metal frame was full of years-old murky water, quite black, which had seeped in through the joints.

There was a succession of Christmas presents that had to be set up on the lawn: some form of paddle tennis, with the ball attached to an upright pole; back yard cricket with a metal wicket, for which our yard wasn't big enough; and a shuttlecock game with a net and two poles.

Little by little, age and interest and available spare time meant that the children no longer used the lawn. We had taken out the fruit trees that were here when Grandma and Grandpa had bought the house, making room for the children's needs, and now the sad and inevitable cycle gave us back the space for other needs. We have fruit trees again.

We still have the machines: bike after bike after bike. A new bike to cope with a growing boy; a new bike to replace a stolen bike; a new bike to replace a bike becoming a safety hazard; a new bike to replace the one on which the brakes had failed, projecting John straight into a wall; and lately, a new bike for Andrew to go to university. He will probably try to beat John's record time from North Terrace to home.

Is the back yard silent now? Or empty? Not at all. When we built a new back verandah a year ago, the boys began to fill it up with a new kind of ironmongery. The boys are in a body-building phase, and late afternoons, early evening, weekends, they work out on the weights and the other equipment. I can hear them: the sound comes indoors where I am reading or working, or floats down into my vegetable garden. Clank. Clank. It's like living in a giant cutlery drawer.

Our needs change as we grow older; the paraphernalia we support ourselves with in our back yards changes as we do, as the children become adults and the adults move on to retirement. I hope the Martian explorers can understand it all.

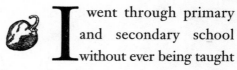I went through primary and secondary school without ever being taught a practical, hands-on subject such as woodwork. My father was a farmer and small shopkeeper, and managed minor repairs all right, but I have no recollection of his ever having a shed or workshop where he kept tools and worked with them.

I never really lived at home again after I was sent to boarding school at twelve, and so I grew to adulthood with very few manual skills and, to be honest, little inclination that way. I had mastered elementary manoeuvres with hammer and screwdriver, and knew how to patch a wall and prepare a room for painting.

I married a woman whose father had been a builder all his life, and could turn his hand to carpentry, tiling, bricklaying, electrical repairs, plumbing, and so on. When we were first married, he worked part-time and so was usually available to patch something up, put in a window, or whatever. Later, when we moved in with him, he did all the repairs. This saved us a lot of money we didn't have to spend on tradespeople.

Giovanni is a man who cannot bear to be idle, and has worked hard all his life. His oldest brother had wanted to send him to university, but he preferred working to staying at school, and before the First World War he was working in Austria with a building team from his town.

When war came, his province was overrun by the Austrian and German armies, and eventually he was called up in the Italian Army. He was in the Alpini – the mountain troops – and saw some active service in the mountains between Italy and Austria. He was eighteen when the war ended; there was no work in Friuli, and he joined building teams again and worked in both France and Germany on some of the rebuilding that followed the war. He remembers working in Nancy, Metz, and Strasbourg, where he learnt to speak French. We still have a book by Lysle, *Metodo Accelerato Razionale per Imparare la Lingua Francese*, which he used to help him learn.

Then he decided to go to Argentina, where another of his family had emigrated. He had his passport ready when he received a letter that had been wrongly delivered to him. It was for someone else in another quarter who had an identical name (a common problem in his town). It was from an Italian who had come to South Australia and was working in Loxton.

This letter amusingly described a South Australian country town on Sunday as seen by a European, but also told its unintended reader that there was work available in Australia. There wasn't much in his home province of Friuli, which traditionally has been a focus of emigration from Italy.

So he came to Australia in 1928, and found work straightaway at Nuriootpa, where he built the brickworks chimney that still stands on the northern side of the town (using a book to work out what to do). Later he moved to Clare, where he ran his own brickworks, and after the Second World War sponsored a string of Italian migrants who came to the town to work with him.

This is the active, practical man with whom I (who have no practical skills to speak of) have shared the yard and shed for over twenty years.

When I saw how my son John loved spending his days with Giovanni in the shed, before he started school, I had high hopes that the skills I had never gained would be acquired by my children.

John, and later Andrew, banged around with hammer and nails, played with wood shavings, and had a good time. They loved their grandfather – he was like a Pied Piper to all the neighbourhood children, always talking to them and listening to them – and Emma and the boys used to spend a lot of time in his room, talking to him, playing his records, eating his peanuts, watching television (we couldn't control the quality of what they watched with him, the way we did in our living room in those days). They begged for more time before they had to have a bath or go to bed, and they had an ally who pleaded subversively on their behalf. We were rather disturbed sometimes by the bloodthirsty calls that seemed to accompany their favourite television entertainment – wrestling – but in spite of a heavy dose of it none of them developed an interest in scripted drama.

I noticed as the years passed that John and Andrew went to the shed less and less, which was understandable once they started at school; but I also noticed with some sadness that they hadn't learnt any of the skills I hoped they might learn.

Though they had tried to do things with Grandpa in the shed, something went wrong. Giovanni isn't a teacher. His English is perfect, but he is not good at explaining how to do the practical things he does so easily. He loses patience very quickly when he sees someone doing something stumblingly that he can do quickly, and he prefers to move in and finish the job rather than teach the other person how to do it.

He would do anything for us, but what we find a little disconcerting is that he always knows a better/cheaper/quicker way of doing something, and in the past often said so. I find all this totally understandable in a clever, self-starting, independently minded person who has worked for himself for much of his life.

Carpentry Lesson

Between Giovanni
at seventy-five
and John
at four-and-three-quarters
(he's *not* four)
there is a sweet
and busy morning
made of hammer and nails.

There are no scales
over my eyes.
I rue my own
thumbed illiteracy
with file and plane
and pliers, but cannot
read the grain of wood
with any sureness
such as my son draws
from that moving cloud
of dust and questions
rattling in the shed.

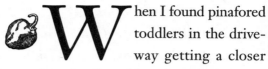When I found pinafored toddlers in the driveway getting a closer look at our lion and patting it, and heard excited conversations with oohing and pointing, I became aware that the lion had become an icon in the district.

Then we started getting responses to directions, such as 'Ah, you mean the house with the lion'. Icon and landmark, now.

Our lion statue is less than life-size but still impressively big. The pose is seated but erect. The colour, which used to be sandy, is these days a rich brown. It cannot be seen quite so easily from the road now, because as Grandpa grew older and spent more of his time in his room, he moved the lion. Once it was in a bare patch in front of the sitting room window, easily seen from the footpath. Now it is in front of his bedroom window, and is screened from the road by a scruffy shrub that gives his room shade in the afternoons.

The lion was made by Arturo Comelli, Tina's uncle. Arturo was a cousin of Tina's mother, from the small town of Nimis near the city of Udine. Arturo did an apprenticeship as a monumental mason when he left school, and later an art course at the Professional School in Nimis. When he came to Australia he also studied sculpture at the South Australian School of Mines. In Italy, Arturo had been a follower of the Fascist patriot, poet and adventurer Gabriele D'Annunzio. He came to Australia in 1926, on the *Città di Genova*, and for much of his life made his living through his art. This included some commissions for sculptures and decorations for churches, some paintings and sculptures, fountains, and a wide range of garden pots and statuary. His commercial products were of good quality; his best personal paintings included some exotic and surreal pieces. He believed in putting his art on public view, and filled his front garden with all sorts of wonderful (and some weird) things. I was familiar with the range of them long before I had met him, for in the late 1940s and early 1950s, when I was at Sacred Heart College, I used to see them from the Anzac Highway buses, in the front garden of a house on the northern side of the Highway, opposite the Keswick Barracks. This was very close to Adelaide's great pop art work, the huge Claude Neon sign. He called his business 'Wonderland Artworks' and it stayed on the site until 1964, when he moved. After this, the whole strip of houses was bulldozed or converted for small businesses.

The large statue of St Francis of Assisi and the Crucified Christ, in the grounds of the church of St Francis of Assisi at Newton, a few kilometres north-east of the city centre, is an Arturo Comelli statue.

He was an active member of the Italian club Fogolar Furlan, a club for northern Italians from the region of Friuli–Venezia Giulia, and wrote poetry in the Furlan dialect, which is a fairly impenetrable language even to an Italian speaker, since it is said to have Celtic as well as Romance components. In its written form it looks more like a Slavic language, with many words ending in consonants, and a range of accent marks. There are half a million speakers of it in Italy. Arturo read his poetry passionately to anyone who would stop and listen, including to me, who didn't understand his English, and knew no Italian, let alone Furlan.

For a short time during the Second World War Arturo Comelli was interned in Loveday Internment Camp, having been caught up in the fairly widespread arrests of Italian citizens. Doubtless his enthusiasm for D'Annunzio led to his being placed on someone's list. At the same time, Australian–Italian soldiers called Scala, Scarpetta, and Scarrabelotti were among those taken as prisoners-of-war in Singapore. In Loveday he occupied himself with sculpture, using mallee, and ran classes in drawing and wood carving. It is believed that he was freed after some visiting dignitary saw the quality of his work.

This was the man who made the lion, a lovely, generous, passionate, idiosyncratic and eccentric man – *sui generis*, one of a kind, sometimes locked away behind his own difficulties with English, but expressing himself freely through his work. If he hadn't had to support himself through garden statuary, there's no telling what he would have done with his art.

He always exhibited in the *Advertiser* Art Exhibition, and sold pieces. I remember one year, when he was in hospital, helping his daughter to deliver a huge and hefty sculpture to the exhibition.

The splendid lion in our front garden was a gift from Arturo Comelli to my parents-in-law. It has moved with them from house to house.

There are a dozen planter pots in the yard that are part of his commercial output, pots with a good line and well made. There are the flamingos, life-size and graceful, with a concrete base to anchor them, slender legs made of steel rods with a coating of concrete, sculptured feathers, and an intelligent head at an interesting angle. We have four, or did at last count, wandering in our shrubbery, standing guard by the fish pond and, for a few years when Giovanni had one of his wilder inspirations, standing sentinel on the concrete slab overhang above the front bedroom window. It is Giovanni who keeps these birds painted.

We still have two of Arturo's Madonna bookends, heavy enough for a row of encyclopedias but with the face of the Madonna on the outside so elegant, so serene, with classical features and the headdress sculptured so that the cloth seems to fall as lightly as in reality. More than the lion, certainly more than the rather kitsch flamingos, these bookends tell me how good he was as an artist.

We lost his best Madonna, which he made for us as a wedding present. She was a statue of the Madonna, slim and elegant, standing about 80 centimetres high, finished like the bookends with an almost metallic green colour in the concrete. We lost it to Addolorata, a cleaner we employed when we had no children, lived in a flat and were both working. She broke it by accident, and cried forever about it, not about being clumsy, not about our loss, but about the sin of breaking a statue of Mary.

We used to have a garden seat that had two ends made by Arturo, but over the years the wooden seat deteriorated and we pulled it apart. What we have left are the two ends, the front of each a clever sculpture with sturdy legs to take the weight of the seat. What I am fascinated by are the creatures themselves that Arturo invented for the seat. Andrew says they remind him of lions, but they are nothing like our impressive realistic lion. They have wide grinning mouths full of regular but not sharp teeth, and large almond-shaped eyes to which Giovanni has given a devilish glint by painting them white with a tiny black pupil. There is a small crest on the top of the head but without any distinguishing feather or fur markings.

Something about them suggests that the sculptor probably had a classical model in mind, and certainly there are elements of some Greek griffins in their shape, something of the sphinx about them, though this is belied by the stance, which turns the bodies into legs for a seat, for the sphinx is static and these are dynamic.

The intense triangularity of their heads makes them look in some ways like antique gargoyles based on a lynx (I have seen pictures of some which are in the Vatican) and in other ways like some Egyptian animal-gods. Perhaps they are chimaeras. Tina says she has always assumed that they were based on some creature from classical mythology.

Then there was the dog. Life-size, life-like, conventional, black and white – an Australian sheepdog without a doubt. I think Arturo made an attempt at a statue of just about every animal (in his front yard there was an emu-based rocking statue complete with seat, saddle and reins). The dog was another of his presents to Giovanni and Maria, and we had it on the front verandah for many years after we moved into the house. Unfortunately, we never took any steps to secure it to the verandah, such as anchoring its feet in a cement slab.

One night it was stolen from us. It was stolen by someone fairly strong, because I could only just lift it off the ground. There has always been plenty of gnome-napping in Adelaide, but there were no ransom notes for our dog, and it didn't turn up in any obvious places such as on the university lawns.

I did report the theft to the local police station, described the loss as a dog, told the constable how long we had had it, its age, and so on, and only at the end did I drop in casually the information that it was a concrete statue of a dog. To my chagrin the policeman didn't even comment.

My father-in-law Giovanni is a man of many skills and ingenious ideas, and always has the last word on anything someone else has made. That is why Arturo Comelli's lion has eyes now. The original statue had deep unfilled cavities as eyes, but Giovanni went one better. The eyes he installed are bright, almost sinister blue, ringed with bright orange. He has done this with two short pieces of orange electrical conduit and two blue marbles.

These eyes follow me around the garden.

Archaeology of the Suburban Dream

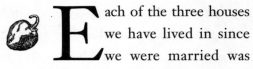

Each of the three houses we have lived in since we were married was built before the Second World War, and our present house, the oldest of the three, was built in the 1920s when this part of the suburb was developed.

Garbage collection seems to have followed housing development by some years in new suburbs, if I am to believe the evidence that I have found under the ground.

I knew when we bought our first house from Mrs Pedlar that her husband had died there after a long illness. When I started to prepare the garden for my first crop of vegetables, I started to find reminders of his illness buried in the yard. There were medicine bottles, some still with labels and therefore fairly recent; there were medicine droppers and syringes used for injections; and in one collection there was even a pair of old spectacles, broken by my spade. Perhaps it was too hard for Mrs Pedlar to throw such intimate and painful things in the bin. We all find it hard to imagine that someone else will use the place we love differently from the way we have done, and Mrs Pedlar's yard was a wild place of unpruned trees and patches of couch grass. She probably thought that what she buried there was safely at rest.

When we moved into our present house, there was a

shed of some antiquity close to the house. It was about a metre from the side fence, and in that space there grew a scraggly purple hibiscus reaching leggily for the light. There were a few acanthus plants that subversively came under the fence from the Bornholms', and still do.

The acanthus were thriving. These are plants that tolerate poor soil and shade, and have to put up with a ridiculous name, since they are known as bear's breeches or Biblical lily. Though these names are laughable, the acanthus has a place in art, for its leaves have such ornamental serrations that since Greek times the shape has been used in two and three-dimensional decorative art.

When we removed the old shed, we put in some filling and let the lawn grow over the space. A few years later, I spent some time creating a garden bed along that side of the yard. I marked out a bed about 1.5 metres deep and all the way to the clothes line and delimited it with old railway sleepers.

Tina and I selected shrubs to plant in the space, and I set to work to get rid of the scanty lawn grasses, dig it over, and sink the holes for the shrubs to be planted in.

About half the section I was working in was the area that had been between the old shed and the fence, and here I started to discover the past, in large quantities.

The first thing I found was a broken bottle, and I cut my hand on it. There were dozens of broken bottles, and some smaller ones unbroken. Some of them had been sunk into the ground in old kerosine tins, which were falling apart with rust.

There was kitchen rubbish such as tin cans, bits of broken crockery, a bent knife, bottle tops, and the occasional broken piece of equipment. I remember parts of what looked like an egg whisk, and a dented colander.

Getting rid of this rubbish – carefully – held up my work for days. There was a sort of modern casualness about the way the former owners had buried what they did not want. I became very careful when I dug up one, and then a second, partly filled bottle of phenyl. One unlabelled, sealed bottle with a little liquid still in it looked like a spirits of salts bottle.

In other parts of the yard, the problem didn't exist as it did there. However, there were plenty of pieces of broken glass and plates in the vegetable garden, and stones everywhere.

We've been here over twenty years now, and our own lives are turning up in the garden. Take marbles, for instance. When our children were small, marbles were sold in little bags with draw-string ties, gaudily labelled 101 MARBLES. Why 101, I wonder, and did anyone ever count? My sons must have had five or six of these bags, and they all disappeared somewhere. I've certainly found some of them among the capsicums and chives.

Other recent additions to the unwanted underground treasure have been ring-pull tops of bottles, the plastic casing of mettwurst, the plastic packing of headache capsules, old band-aids. These are the sorts of non-biodegradable odds and ends that family members throw casually into the kitchen scraps. They then end up in the garden via the compost heap. Recently I found half a green toy soldier, rifle still at the shoulder arms position.

The only valuable thing I ever found was something I had lost a fortnight before and had been desperate to find. This was my wedding ring. I had been ill and had lost weight, and was collecting vegetables one evening when my ring fell off my finger. All my searching was to no avail. It was obviously in the vegetable garden somewhere, and I thought I knew where. Two weeks later, among the carrots, I saw its gleam.

Ritual

There is a ritual involved with visitors to our house: the walk around the garden. Guests who come to dinner after dark are spared this tour, but relatives, close friends, work colleagues who come to lunch, all get shown the garden.

This is when Fausto tells me about planting by the moon; when Jordan offers me all the cow manure I can collect from his place; when herbs are envied and carrots admired. This is when I get told I am not pruning the tomatoes hard enough, or that the lettuces need thinning out. This is when treaties and arrangements are made to exchange seeds and cuttings and roots.

However, my strongest and saddest memories of the garden-walking ritual are of my father. In the years after my mother died, he came to tea once or twice a week. At first he drove himself, until we had to ban him from driving after he moved out of a side street into the side of a car he didn't see. For a while, he came by bus and I drove him home, until he grew too frail. After that, I used to pick him up after work.

My father was a taciturn man, and I'm not a good conversationalist myself. After he'd talked to the children, and let them tell him about their exploits in sport at school, and fed them white peppermints from his cardigan pocket, I used to take him for a walk around the garden. He walked slowly, and talked little. I used to ask his advice, show off my successes, and we'd reminisce a lot.

I was the only one of the four children who lived close to him. I had never been close to him before, and had spent all my adolescence away from home, but in these years when he was on his own I came to know him well, and missed him very much when he died. I wrote the poem 'My Father, Visiting' about a year after he died when, late one afternoon in the garden, I recalled his presence strongly and vividly. I sat down that night and wrote for hours to recapture some of the feelings I had.

My Father, Visiting

1.
I walk this garden at his, my father's, pace,
two weak legs and a dependent stick beside.
He remembers the rows of crinkled lettuce he sees
and talks, but raspily now, of snails and bait.

I have grown slowly into these, my fruitful rows
of carrots and zucchini, into contradictory skills
of growing green he did not dare, and daring not
his flags of flowers coaxed out of the sun.

Could I step aside and see the lad, the man,
escort my patient father round the paths, who'd wish
rather the peach-shade in the cool, and not this pride
of success with carrots and the steady aubergine?

I might stay in the walnut's depth of gloom, and see
the filling of time, the old man empty of all but bone
and necessary words, the filling of time, come to lunch
on New Year's Eve, and hope, or pray, whatever we do.

2.

Portrait: across the table
fussing with gravy, with meat
not tender enough for teeth.
His minimum words support
our conversations, ease along
the ordinary days we list
for him. Across the table
I see his hands are alive
with brown and purple scars.
The sun picks at them always
and they crust into salty scale.
He grew the moustache the year
my mother died; it filled
in time. It said: Yes,
I am myself – before we all
propped him at table
in our successive homes,
slower now, week after week.

3.

To this house of heroes I have brought
this uncomfortable man, across the five suburbs
of our passage clutching his stick, the voice rasp
infrequent as consolation. There are fewer
words between us than before, and he forgets
and I forget what has been really said,

saving the few things that we have to say
for decent intervals. It will be such a day
as every week; he will describe the shopping
and I will talk about the kids. He will grin
about some adventure of his malevolent cat.
Then we will eat, and walk around the garden.
He will read my paper, cough and spit
and hand out peppermints. One of us then
will beat the other to suggest he goes
home to the black cat and the greasy towel
still spread on the back of his favourite chair.

4.
The night is full of lazy sound.
Hear the ridiculous crickets divide
the silence. A stamp of foot
and they all stop.

A golden spider stitches ambition and supper
across a path. The neighbour's sprinkler slides
into twilight to a song of soft rain
on wooden fence.

In my head the shuffle of brown slippers
my father wore; in my head the words we passed
between us, looking for meanings; in my head
no meanings come.

Someone is washing up two doors away.
The far splash of swimmers in back yard pools
survives an intervention of hedge and fence.
I hear my breath

at the side of the house, under the overhang
of jasmine. Silent I am. I wait to walk
around a corner and meet myself, confused,
in slippers brown,

under the cloud of bells and traffic sounds,
the lazy night and voices from over the fence
of swimmers; the crickets close. Some hours ago
I took him home.

5.
Remembering nights I've rung him up.
He's partly deaf and likes the television loud,
and cannot hear the phone. I try again,
and later, again, until at ten o'clock
it's into the car, across five suburbs
all nearly asleep, wondering what I'll find.
He's there, of course; he snores in his chair,
not sprawled dead with his teeth adrift
and the cat of foul temper wanting out.
He grins and mocks my fear, we talk awhile
and share his port. And I drive back.

Bump in the Night

The world is full of noise in the quietness of the night, though Tina, who sleeps well, does not share it with me. I wake up at the slightest sound.

I have a theory that the origin of this difference may lie in ancient gender-roles. Any family's line has survived because somewhere in the dark past have been ancestors with survival skills better than those of some of their fellows. I like to imagine that in my ancestry are some of those smart prehistoric fellows who were able to wake instantly when the sabre-tooth tiger or whatever threatened the cave. If you could wake up at the first slight sound and were strong enough to beat off the tiger, your genes would be more likely to survive into the next generation. If you couldn't, lucky tiger, unlucky you.

I don't seem to have much of this ancestral tower of strength in me, except for the alertness at night. Everything wakes me up.

As the children grew and started to go out at night and sometimes come in late, my wakefulness kept track of their arrivals. (When they were young and cried at night, I didn't wake, but Tina did.) It's a selective hearing, because it tunes out the dishwasher, which we usually put on before we go to bed, and the refrigerator, and the hot water system reheating. I do not resent the intrusion of rain on my sleep, for in a dry country there is a great restfulness in being able to lie awake and listen to rain quietly falling.

When I was a child, my parents used to talk of getting late summer rains from 'the tail end of the monsoon'. This was well before the sophisticated weather forecasts we now have; well before television educated us all to the possibilities of moist air bringing rain from the north-west in the train of heavy downpours further north. This steady, almost silent, rain from warm air sometimes reaches Adelaide in late summer, and is the most pleasant of all to listen to.

In spring, the nights fill with the long lonely calls of my quail, and the finches stir and twitter when a wandering cat inspects their cage.

When it is windy, the sound is a plastic container rolling around the yard; a beer can; an empty plastic garden pot; leaves shuffling along the path. Once, the garden umbrella lifted from its hole in the table and carried to the side of the yard.

The possums have no intention of moving out just because the suburbs have moved in. They often bound over the roof on their way from A to B.

Since he had his first scare with his heart, I wake whenever Grandpa, at the front of the house, moves from his room at night.

I've adjusted to and assimilated all the common night noises of our house and garden, except for the burglar. The burglar is that group of noises I do not recognise, which happen in far parts of the house, and send me, with little confidence and a heavy torch, to see what has happened. Nothing ever has, and I pad back to bed, listening carefully.

My greatest night fear is not a noise, but a living thing. We keep bread in the freezer, and keep the freezer in the cubby-house, at the end of the yard, because there is no room in the house. I have unwarily gone down to get a loaf, to thaw so that we can cut lunches, and have run straight into a spider web strung between trellis and tree, across the path. This is a frightening experience, and no rational appraisal makes it better. I think only of a spider dropping straight into my mouth.

In a yard full of trees and trellises, orb-weaving spiders are common, and evening excursions in the yard tingle with fear. I always take the torch with me.

Did You Sleep Well, Dear?

I am all night in a province of thieves
who rob my certainties. Those possums
up in the peach snarl such threats
I've not heard since the cave. Someone's
gate-left-open dog lightly on gravel
growls beside the house, and cats panic
and leap the fence. This is a suburb
sixty years in the making, and still
on the edge of savannah, but if I shut
windows and doors summer will choke
and my wife insist on air, and sleep
again, while my wide eyes awake slip
and dart at the edge of this dark siege.
And the house itself then leaps, cracks bones
up in the roof, closes far doors and drips
in careless bathrooms all the night.

Rain in Summer

It is with some insistence that this rain
will splash dirt onto the green leaves
of lettuce, and will soak full
the left-over nests of spring, and I,
awake in the first rain for months,
hear the sodden slop to the path
of a nest intricate with grass and mud,
fallen from vines beside our room.
And I do not hear, this night,
the hungry rasps of possums in the peach.

Possum Weather

This is possum weather,
when they ease their shadows
out of shadows, ooze from eaves,
run liquid swiftness over guttering,
under verandahs, onto the roof.

They run their races above my head,
they thump and thunder,
come to sudden skids
in and out of my sleep.

The ceiling is fairground,
runway, slippery dip.
They sleep through bright nights
of sunlight, deep
in the only hollows here,
the cavity walls.
So they hide in crevices
between our lives,
dream interrupted dreams
of fruit.

I wonder what they make
of the scraping and lumping
of furniture shifting.
I wonder what they make
of wrestling kids,
of 'Sesame Street' on Two,
and violin practice.

Remember that night
we were new in the house.
We still edged and stepped
like guests around the relics
of other people's lives.
The cup of coffee silence
of children in bed.
Mentally holding hands.

Didn't know we had possums
deep in the walls, asleep,
till we heard them stir.
Little sounds scribbled
behind our backs
in the cooling walls.

Rats, perhaps?
Birds?
And then the race on the roof.
Possums!

One night shortly after,
pulling the blind up,
I saw, perched on the roofline
of next door's shed, a face
of an old crone, inches long,
and stationary, alert,
against the pearl of the sky.

They're what take my grapes;
they spatter and shit mulberries.
My paths are polka-dot purple now.
They leap faster than cats,
gutter to fence to tree,
more of the air than of earth.

I haven't had sultanas any year
except for leavings.

And their skulls are iron,
and their claws for fights.
I remember (it's thirty years
back in dream country now)
at school, the top floor,
three flights up; a possum
caught in the dormitory,
and thirty boys from study
at the blood end of the day.

The baseball bat's a heavy lump,
the cricket bat's as good.
The chase was chaotic and cold,
over the monogrammed quilts,
behind the lockers, wardrobe corners,
shelves and beds. That possum
moved as fast as guilt,
never cowered, broke intelligently,
learnt to duck.

Over and over, wood on bone.
That skull took all our blows.
Bone almost rang like bell.
Every one of us dealt
the undone deaths of bats,
bloody-minded, twelve years old.

I don't say she defied us.
Defiance is deliberate; she survived.
We never faltered
into the solemnities of myth,
standing around awed,
respecting the cornered beast.
None of that. The last bat
hit as she dodged, leapt
to a ledge, and out a window
fifty feet to the ground.
She picked herself up and ran like hell.

They're tough.
I saw one drag
its bright spilt guts home
once, from a car.

I have a friend Orlando traps them
(illegal, of course) with apples
in a cage; drives to work
at San Remo Macaroni,
drops them off in Rundle Road.
He's repopulating parklands from his street.

I knew where they got in.
In possum weather I waited
till one o'clock, ladder in place,
hammer, nails, and wood.
When the possums slid out
for the Grand Prix on the tiles
and up the trees, I sealed the holes.

They're still around, of course.
There's evidence, and no doubt:
the young shoots gone, the stripped bunches,
toothmarks on the peach.

They're welcome.
Nice that something else
(besides the skink and spider)
finds room to live round here.

But they can stay
right off my creeping spine,
out of my walls.

Part Two

Fortress Giovanni

My father-in-law has grown a fig tree between the shed and the cubby-house, in a space that is proving to be too small for it. It has now grown to fill the space completely, and we keep access to shed and cubby open by rigorous pruning of lower growth. Its height is nearly 3 metres now.

The figs – they are small sugar figs – are tasty, and Grandpa proudly brings in little bowls full of them for us to share. He usually gets one of his daughters to make a little jam for him.

Unfortunately, the local blackbirds also find them tasty, and Grandpa refuses to be beaten. Each year, as soon as the fruit sets, he builds Fortress Giovanni.

Across the top of the tree he stretches a huge piece of shade cloth, attached to two long pieces of wood to weigh it down. This goes from Mrs Quarter's fence right across the tree. It covers the whole expanse of the tree between the shed and the cubby. Then he attaches a hanging curtain of shade cloth between the shed and the back fence, between the cubby and the fence (each of these only a metre gap), and yet another curtain about 4 metres long for the gap between the two buildings, with a shade cloth door across the path.

He usually does this without asking for help, unless he is feeling off colour. We come home from work and it has been erected. The figs are supposed to be safe.

The blackbirds still get in. Either evolution or intelligence is at work, but they now know that the way in is to walk – yes, walk – under the drapes of the fortress and then have their way with the fruit.

If the birds are surprised at their depredations, they fly up, trying to get away, and are bamboozled by the black cloth sky that halts them. But they are too high for me or Grandpa to catch. Stalemate. When we go away, they work their way out again, on foot.

There are now so many figs that it doesn't matter if the family of blackbirds that has adopted my garden has a daily feast.

Figs are a good immigrant, adapted well to a dry climate like ours. Our tree survives mostly from the water that runs through the drain behind the shed. However, recently I found a root in the vegetable garden when I was cleaning up after taking out some spent melon vines. To get there it had to travel under a path a metre wide and under the corner of the shed.

My way of discouraging an invasive fig tree root system is regularly to drive in a spade to its full length along whatever line I have decided is the limit.

One of the hardest jobs I have ever had to do was to take out a fig tree. At the first small house we owned were two large, rambling fig trees at the end of the yard, and I was anxious to begin to grow vegetables after a year living in a flat.

The roots were the problem: the woody branches cut and broke easily. Under the ground was a different matter, for the roots curled and twisted in such contortions that there was no simple way to attack the problem. Add to that my newness in the gardening business, equipped with a spade, a small tomahawk, and a saw.

It took forever, over several weekends, and when I had finished I had to dig out couch grass as well; then I had a patch of light sandy soil for my first patch of carrots.

The ancient Romans dedicated the fig tree to Mars (who is better known as the god of war) in his role as a god of agriculture. In Greece, there was Iris, the messenger of the gods, who was offered dried figs and cakes made of wheat and honey (all very healthy) in her shrine at Delos. Given the fast-moving power of the fig in all sorts of folk laxatives, a gift of figs to a messenger god sounds like mythology created by a wit.

Catsday

Morning.
Supervise the blackbirds on the lawn.
Scratch on the door.
Leap up into the dusty fig.
Check the bird cage.
See if the finches are ready to eat.
Scratch in the seedling patch.
Nibble at grass, and leap
and try to catch
a butterfly's shivery twitch by the tap.
Avoid every bee.

Afternoon.
Check up on Grandpa. Check out the shed.
Watch as he planes and saws.
Sniff shavings that smell like forests.
Enter a cupboard of cobwebs.
Hide in the carrots and hope for a bird.
Eat a grasshopper, front half.
Finish off breakfast
and check on the finches again.

Evening.
Know that the light turns lemon
and the day goes sour
and cold.
Watch for the first car home.
Ignore the driver, and greet the car.
Stretch out warm on the bonnet
and sleep, as the engine cools.

Another Learning Experience for Dad

The Great Cat Massacre began in my head
when all three children fed him meat,
and milk, and bits of bread, and then
nursed him and patted him and made him purr

and I

getting good at bitter experience now
knew very well who'd feed him meat
and milk five days hence, and after that,
and pat him not, and kick him out of doors.

Pompey

Pompey is not an appropriate name
for a cat who sprawls all day
in a cool damp trench she's found
among the capsicums.

She's hidden well, and not disturbed
by any hungry scratching bird.

A white cat named for a consul:
I'd expect at least that mice
would be driven away, expect
the sundry thieving birds
to seek out other provinces
and not my ripening grapes.

She has chosen to ignore
historical precedent, and yet
last night something moonlight black
and sounding very mean came in
over the trellises, and screamed
across whatever Rubicon exists
outside there, in the dark.

Cat and Commodore

The cat's eyes shine in the light of my car.

He can spend life slung under a bush
all day, all night, emerging for milk
and meat. He can sleep light sleep.

The swing of the comet cannot confound
the aspirations of cat: the long tail,
as light as froth, swings across stars
and is gone. There is a small zone
of affection and a broad arc
called indifference, provided the meat
comes, and the milk, and cars come home

and the cat can leap up onto the warm
and lie there, hours, long hours, asleep.

Mushrooms

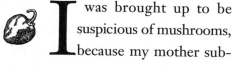I was brought up to be suspicious of mushrooms, because my mother subscribed to the idea that the average eye could not tell the difference between a poisonous mushroom and one that could be eaten. Perhaps she brought this idea from the Huddleston Hills near Crystal Brook, where she grew up. Certainly the arid northern landscapes of Hammond, on the Willochra Plain, where she spent the first years of her married life, rarely produced mushrooms.

Mushrooms and toadstools appear from time to time in our yard. In autumn, there is an arc of small white mushrooms (or toadstools – who knows?) around the base of an evergreen alder. Not a fairy circle, but an arc of about 120 degrees. Underneath a jasmine, under the carport where sunlight never reaches, there has often been a rash of similar mushrooms in untidy clusters, jostling one another for room.

These last for a day or two, and then begin to moulder into a black slimy mess. A few days later the next generation arrives. They are growing only in the area that gets soaked when I water the jasmine. I wonder what they are growing on. On the other side of the fence there used to be a large ash tree – but Peter Bornholm had it taken out. Its roots are still there rotting in the ground, and it may be on this that the mushrooms are growing.

In the closed compost container at the end of the yard delicately shaped, almost transparent little fungi grow sometimes, particularly on discarded marrows. They have a life of less than a day. They look like tiny translucent parasols, with the ribs showing clearly.

The only mushrooms growing in our yard that look at all as if they might be the customary edible mushrooms of the greengrocer's come up on the shady margins of the front lawn. Sometimes they grow to 6 or 7 centimetres in diameter, with dirty brownish-white tops, and last a couple of days.

In my English classes, I always start year eleven poetry with Sylvia Plath's poem 'Mushrooms' to get my students to understand that a poem can be read on more than one level. As well as being about mushrooms, it's a clever and strongly stated political poem.

Some years I have bought a mushroom farm at the supermarket. This is a box full of a growing medium and mushroom spores, and when put in a dark place it produces many dozens of little button mushrooms. It is good to have mushrooms at hand in the shed or in the cupboard, though there is a drawback in having so many at once, and over several weeks, since the family are only occasional mushroom eaters.

History's most famous mushroom eater died from

them. He was the Roman emperor Claudius, who was poisoned by eating the wrong mushrooms in AD 54. For his wife Agrippina, who history says was his poisoner, they were undoubtedly the right mushrooms! She had already dispatched a previous husband by poison, and later poisoned Britannicus, the son of Claudius. The unlovely Agrippina had also persuaded Claudius to pass over Britannicus for the succession as emperor, in favour of her son Lucius Domitius Ahenobarbus, who is better known as Nero.

Since there are several dozen species of mushroom poisonous to human beings, and since Agrippina's character was well known to all of her contemporaries, Claudius could have been a little more careful when his wife smiled and said 'Fungus, darling'.

For Andrew

For six days my son watched
with nine-year-old wonder
a sturdy mushroom that shouldered
aside the bitumen and bulged
into being beside the road.

He sprinkled it daily
with curiosity and close
inspection, and it strained
like a globe up out of
black gravel and tar.

On the seventh day it should
have rested, taken the sun
full on its back. My boy
saw instead a powdered corpse
under the wheels of a car.

Willow, Willow

This is not a slow-growing tree.

'The willow will buy a horse before the oak will pay for a saddle.' This English proverb, recorded in the 17th century, demonstrates succinctly the speed with which the willow will grow and produce saleable wood to the owner's profit.

The willow tree has been thoroughly assimilated into Australian landscapes in the better-watered parts of the country, and can be seen along creeks right through south-eastern Australia. It provides green brightness to landscapes in summer, and its distinctive yellowish-tinted dryness when its leaves are gone creates a poetic tracery in winter. Where sheep and cattle graze around willows, they will eat the foliage when there is nothing else, and so it is quite common to see willows with a kind of bobbed haircut, trimmed evenly to the height the animals can reach. Where there are no animals to eat the leaves, the soil underneath the tree is swept clean by the always moving fronds of the willow.

The willow that is common in Australian landscapes is *Salix babylonica*, the weeping willow, a native of China. Why *babylonica*, I wonder? By the waters of Babylon they sat down and wept. Perhaps it was named by a well-read botanist.

Willows and water are well matched. When Claude Monet developed his water garden at Giverny, in which he planted the water lilies he painted so often, he put willows around the edge. A 20th century gardener has planted willows in the garden of the Villa Malcontenta, which Palladio built in 1560; a traveller on the River Brenta in Italy can still see the classical outline of the house, but it is softened by the delicacy of the willow foliage.

When Tina's parents moved into our present house, just after we were married, the yard was bare. I, unfortunately as it turned out, knew very little about gardens and trees then, and that is how we came to buy two weeping willows as a birthday present for Tina's mother. She planted them both, one in the back yard, well away from the house, the other in the middle of the front garden.

Four years later, when she had died and we had come to the house, we found we had two willows to look after, one small and sickly, the other in extremely good health.

The sickly willow that had been planted in the front garden had never had the chance to put down the sort of root system a willow needs, because where it had been planted was a fish pond, now buried under the lawn, which Giovanni had filled in soon after he moved in, while Maria was making a visit to Italy. He had changed the levels of the front garden and the old pond was well underground. The tree never grew above 2 metres high, and stayed a thin, yellowing thing.

The tree in the back yard was different, but didn't present a problem – yet! We built on a suite of rooms, and this meant that the willow was now a lot closer to the house. The house had moved, but so had the willow, spreading sideways fairly quickly. The shade it provided was most welcome in summer, and when the leaves fell I got many barrow loads for composting.

Time passed. The tree reached the edge of Grandpa's room and started dragging its fronds across the eaves and dropping leaves into the gutter. We were having second thoughts about this tree.

Then we discovered that it had worked out where the vegetable garden was and had sent exploring roots in under the lettuces and carrots. There was plenty of water there through the hot season, and willows of full size take up and transpire tonnes of water every week in hot weather. It had to go.

Willow

This willow is kelp in currents
sucked and surged by a lazy sea.

This willow is crazy tails of crazy sheep.

I can see frantic tassels twitch
on the boobs of go-go dancers
in Brobdingnag, after the eighth drink.

I think I am prisoner of this tree,
its slave. I am programmed annually
to rake its million leaves. Anyone need
some mulch? I can deliver
twenty-five barrow-loads this year.

This is a monster beached in my yard.
Its hair is green, its huge hump
is visible back yards away.

And then the wind. The tree succumbs
slave to the air about it; watch it
thresh and lash and bound.

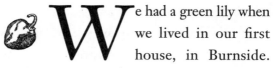We had a green lily when we lived in our first house, in Burnside. One of my aunts gave it to us, and we put it where she suggested, in a damp shady place, where it thrived.

The flower from this lily had a green hood and a paler green stamen, with a strong sweet smell that could be smelt from yards away. In it was all the sensuality of a warm, rich summer night. Put a flower in one room and the scent filled two or three.

It didn't have a name. When I potted several of them and took them to a fete, I thought they were elephant's ears. No, John, they're not, a colleague told me, as she bought one.

They are easy to move from house to house, and virtually indestructible. I've seen a trunk lying in the sun for three months still not dried out, and sending out shoots and putting down roots when planted in the soil. I create new plants by breaking a trunk into several pieces and nearly burying each. The plant itself sends out side shoots, which quickly develop into new plants.

For years we grew them in the shady side garden of our present house, and then we rearranged things and didn't need them any more. Rather than not have them when we might decide to move, or reorganise again, I put them in a temporary parking place behind the shed, where they stay alive, produce a few flowers, but aren't thriving particularly well because it is too dry in summer.

Then we found the name when Tina bought a book about scented plants for Australian gardens. Our green lily is a cunjevoi, botanical name *Alocasia macrorrhiza*.

It is a native, from the rainforests of northern New South Wales and Queensland, and also through South-East Asia. Aborigines used to eat the tuberous rootstock, but it is poisonous unless it has first been cooked. I have often wondered what series of trial and error, and at whose expense, led to the conclusion that some things which are poisonous uncooked are safe if cooked or boiled or macerated.

Consider the toxic fruits of the cycad. In North Queensland the Aborigines removed the outer cover, pounded the kernels, dried them in the sun for three or four hours, left them (in a woven bag) in running water for a few days, and then in stagnant water for a few more before pounding them into a paste and baking this under ashes similar to the way damper is cooked. How did someone work that out, when avoidance is a normal reaction to something which poisons the eater? A mystery!

The flowers, leaves and rootstock of the cunjevoi are all poisonous. The juice can damage the eyes, and even handling the flowers can leave poisons on the fingers to burn the lips.

Oddly, the name *cunjevoi* is also the Aboriginal name of a sea creature called the sea squirt, used for bait by fishermen.

If we had known from the start that the cunjevoi was a cunjevoi, we would have called it that and assimilated the name. After over twenty years we can only call it the green lily.

The Green Lily

How unsettling it is, to discover the name
of a plant I have dealt with for years:
divided and mulched, potted and given away,
donated to fetes and moved from corner
to coveted corner, and always it's been
'that green lily from Nell'. There's a name now
I cannot pronounce, and a page in a book.
We bring its flower inside: the green scent
captures whole rooms. It lingers for days.
None of this needed a catalogue's burden of name.

How unsettling. As if the loving wife
of one's life had turned one evening
to say: Now I can tell you my name.
As if the green lily children had grown
new faces, not at all like mine, and worn
shop assistants' badges saying: Smile!
As if someone hammered up a large square brass
on the picket fence around my privacy
and painted on it names I cannot own.
As if the lily's scent was captured, bottled,
analysed, all the belonging taken out,
and formulae derived, and given just a name.

Mr Belvedere

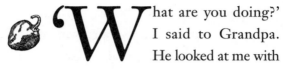'What are you doing?' I said to Grandpa. He looked at me with a smile. 'I'm building you something nice.'

After the willow tree was gone, we had planted a grape vine at the back of the house, and bought some perma-pine posts. Grandpa spent a couple of weeks in his spare time building a trellis with these over which, eventually, the grape vine was supposed to spread.

A year later the modifications began. His 'something nice' started to take shape on top of the trellis. It was being built of old pieces of sheet iron, old boards, old iron pipes: a floor laid above the trellis, a railing put around it.

'What is it for?' I asked.

'The children will be able to come up here and sunbathe, or read,' he said. He had noticed them sunbathing on the trampoline.

The construction – contraption – was not a pretty sight, but there were plenty of reasons not to object. Grandpa needed physical activity to keep busy and active; he had been very generous to us in helping pay for the additions; and he was an instant baby sitter whenever we needed him. He was a warm and gentle man who couldn't, in his old age, be dumped into a room and left there. We knew he needed to be allowed to make decisions for himself, even when we didn't really like the result.

Finally he built a set of stairs, with a hand rail on one side made from old metal electrical conduit from a demolished building. The steps were strong, but not identical.

The 'something nice' he had built for us was ready, and the children loved it. Grandpa put one of the Comelli flamingos up there, to look out serenely over the yard, and Emma carried up a steel garden chair to lounge in and read. There was still enough room for another one to lie and sunbake.

When the Grand Prix was held in Adelaide, we had a balcony view of the aerobatics and the parachute drops and the displays of precision flying by RAAF teams. The structure was strong enough and big enough to hold all of us, and we all used it. This good view was some compensation for living so close to the Festival of Petrol and its intolerable noise.

We got a better view than most of our neighbours did of the increasingly frequent fireworks displays put on in Adelaide as bread and circuses became the style of government. We also got a better-than-average view of our neighbours.

Then we remembered the name for what he had built. We had our very own belvedere. Grandpa didn't recognise the word when it was pronounced in the English way, but when I said it in approximate Italian he knew what it was.

The word *belvedere* in Italian means a beautiful view. In architecture it is a structure with a roof, but open on one or more sides, built usually as part of the main building, but sometimes as a separate structure. Its purpose is to allow the idle inhabitants of palazzos and villas to enjoy the view.

The Renaissance Italians who commissioned belvederes to be built in their new villas would have looked on something more inviting than a series of back yards and a skylarking daredevil doing aerobatics in a small propeller-driven plane.

A Tale of Two Bird Baths

Each year, my father-in-law asks Tina if there is anything special she would like for Christmas, and then they go off to buy it.

One year it was a bird bath Tina wanted. There are always birds in the garden, chasing nectar, on their way to the grapes, parrots driving towards the Bornholms' apples, doves working over the lawn for the seed I throw out when I clean out the feed trays in the bird cages.

Tina had intended the bird bath for the front lawn, but I had memories of the way in which the Comelli concrete dog had been stolen, despite its weight. I suggested that the bird bath be put temporarily at the back of the house until I had worked out how to fix it *in situ*.

Good intentions deliver a lot of delay. It is still behind the house.

Christmas morning came. There was to be a formal visitation and unwrapping at eleven-thirty when the relatives arrived, on their way to wherever. They did not arrive en famille, since the older cousins no longer lived at home. First there were two female voices coming through the front hall, and then, about five minutes later, much struggling and puffing along the side of the house, as two strapping young men delivered the second bird bath of the day. This was for Grandpa, and was identical to the one Grandpa had bought for Tina. It had come from the same garden shop, where at least one salesperson knew the connections between the two families, but she had been at lunch when the second of the two buyers had arrived.

On Boxing Day Grandpa installed his bird bath in the front garden outside his window, and Tina's stayed on the back lawn. After a couple of weeks of seeing not a single bird in his bird bath, which was just outside (and probably too close to) the window from which he surveys the avenue in the afternoons, he gave it to his grandson for his garden.

Our bird bath didn't attract a bird in the first site we had it, until we moved it further from the house. Then the blackbirds and the sparrows started to dunk themselves in it. Unfortunately we couldn't see it well, and so I moved it a last time, to a place where we could see and enjoy it from Tina's study and from mine, as well as from the back door, and we are rewarded every evening by the bird ablutions. It seems to be happily placed, near two fruit trees, in whose branches the birds first sit and check that they will be safe, before bathing.

Blackbirds (sometimes six or seven at a time) create a great spray, as they sit right in the water and beat their wings fast, as if revving up. Sparrows land lightly on the edge, check their safety again, jump in feet first for a couple of seconds, duck under, and then fly out to shake themselves on the tree. Other visitors are turtle doves, starlings, wagtails, and piping shrikes. Each has its own style of drinking and bathing. The turtle doves look faintly ridiculous as they jump in with a sort of fat-person plop, duck their breast feathers in the water, and jump out again.

The bird bath is so much used that I have to fill it up three or four times a day in the summer holidays.

Joseph Addison said, 'I value my garden more for being full of blackbirds than of cherries, and very frankly give them fruit for their songs'. I would rather native birds than blackbirds, and I resent losing fruit to any birds, but I certainly enjoy a garden full of living such as I see when the blackbirds rev up in the bird bath.

Mrs Quarter and Me

**M**rs Quarter was a great disappointment to my mother-in-law Maria during the few years she lived here before her early death.

Maria was a friendly, generous woman who believed she should get to know her neighbours and engage with them regularly in conversation and gifts of produce across the fence.

Mrs Quarter wanted none of that, was decidedly unfriendly, and maintained an Arctic distance.

We rarely saw her, but heard the sound of her air conditioner as soon as it grew hot, and could hear her sprinkler on the little back lawn of her unit. We heard her voice talking to her son when he came to visit.

In our early years, the end of the yard was bare of shed, cubby-house, fig tree and bird cages: a kind of wilderness kept for growing those vegetables which took a lot of space, particularly marrows and broad beans. It was also where we had our bonfires.

Getting rid of trees then involved burning, on a scale too big for an incinerator. That was how we dealt with the willow, and with the remains of three old almond trees that Grandpa had taken out but left propped grotesquely at the end of the yard.

Now, in the interests of cleaner air, we are prevented by law from burning in bonfires or incinerators, and that's a good thing.

Mrs Quarter never spoke to me about her worries about bonfires. She let me know by attacking me with water. One day, as I was burning some twiggy rubbish, she turned her tap on full blast and hosed both me and the bonfire over the fence.

Words ensued. She was worried that the fire would catch on to the eaves of her unit. This was 2 metres from the fence, and my fire was 5 metres the other side. Trigonometry wasn't allowed to spoil a good argument.

It's a bit hard to reconcile with a neighbour hidden from view by a fence too high for either party to see over. The normal conciliatory courtesies of greeting were of no use in this situation.

Then the footballs started, and she was scared for her windows and her pot plants. Quite rightly, too, for my son John had a long, strong kick and a short memory for my warnings. Sometimes it seemed as if the most important thing in John's life was to kick the ball further than ever before.

Over the fence meant out. John could scale the fence, but there were no footholds to get back again, and so he had to run around the block. Sometimes he left his football there until Mrs Quarter threw it back, sometimes he dared go across.

Not that this happened often, but Mrs Quarter threatened to keep the ball prisoner, and I did my best to talk to her about John's enthusiasm and lack of bad intentions, and tried to get her to remember what active boys can be like. Her son spoke to me about her fears, and we banned the football in the yard and started going around to the local park.

Blue-tongue Lizard

Peter Frangiosa sold Andrew a lizard, when Andrew was in year five. Giovanni already had a cage for it, cobbled together out of chicken wire and some of the various odd pieces of aluminium he had collected over the years. He had made it when we had a white rabbit, and it was designed to be moved from place to place in the garden so that the rabbit could do its part in keeping the grass short. The blue-tongue was installed, and Andrew set about learning what he needed to do to feed the creature and keep it healthy.

A fortnight later, the blue-tongue escaped. We searched for it over several days before we gave up, and the cage was hoisted up behind the shed once more to gather cobwebs. Our best guess was that one of the roaming local dogs had probably found the wandering lizard and dealt with it.

A couple of years later, the lizard, or a lizard, was back in residence with us. Tina saw it first, when she was hanging out some washing, sunning itself near the clothes line. By the time she told me, it had moved, but various members of the family saw it from time to time at the back of the yard. Then one day I heard a rustling in the shed, behind a stack of old doors and pieces of plyboard, and a few days later as I came down the path I saw its nose sticking out from the shed door. As I approached it hurried out of sight, and when I entered the shed there was the same rustling again behind the stack of junk.

We assumed that the lizard had made itself a hideaway there, and often saw it in the back half of the yard. But the shed is bitterly cold in winter, and has a concrete floor; so I presumed it didn't spend its winters there.

As it turned out, it did have a permanent home, and the shed must merely have been one of the places it explored and foraged in. Eventually we found a small hole scratched at the side of the cubby-house and saw the blue-tongue emerge from it. It has used that place ever since, and when the little garden patch alongside the cubby is cultivated and the hole gets covered over, it is scratched open again within a couple of days, unless it is winter when the lizard seems to hibernate.

I've even seen the lizard inside the cubby-house, where there is a resident population of many insects. However, I suspect that the real attraction of the cubby may be the freezer. Years ago, in another house, we bought a freezer far too big for us, which we kept in my study for a while after we moved to this house, and then exiled to the cubby, where it has purred away for over twenty years without pause. It must be warm underneath the freezer, where the motor runs, and I have often seen our lizard in there. I know that there is also a population of snails under there, for they crawl in from the garden, and the lizard must make some of its diet on these.

As for the rest of the food it needs, I imagine that slaters, of which I am host to several million, form a large part of its daily requirements. I wonder does it like millipedes? Nothing else in Australia seems to like these nasty little Portuguese immigrants.

After assuming for several years that there was this one, perhaps lonely, bachelor or spinster lizard in the yard, I saw one day a slim-line youngster, also a blue-tongue, on the path outside Giovanni's room. This path is a narrow one, between our house and the neighbour's yard, and since our side boundary abuts the neighbour's rear boundary, there are, on the other side of the fence here, a wood heap, a pile of railway sleepers, a huge and ancient mulberry tree, an old children's swimming pool, and a higgledy-piggledy collection of junk. This con-glomeration of hiding places must be the home of more blue-tongues, since one lizard does not a family make.

My elderly neighbour at the end of the yard, Mrs Rosemead, poured friendly scorn on me when I said how comforting it was that there were still lizards around even though this part of Toorak Gardens has been a suburban street since the early 1920s. 'Oh, Douglas used to have lizards as pets when he was a small boy. Some of them got away.' End of ecological wonder.

A few days later: 'John, I've found some lizard eggs in my garden. Would your boys like to try to hatch them?' Well, I would like to try, and so I took a slightly interested boy with me, and a small container, and we were led to the front lawn and left to collect the eggs. Mrs Rosemead went back inside. They were small, dirty white, spherical, and suspiciously light in weight. There were also several hundred of them. They had been laid in a plastics factory, were made of styrofoam, and had blown in from the road where they had been disgorged from someone's garbage bin when the morning collection had been picked up.

End of experimental hatching of lizard eggs.

Nevertheless, somewhere in my garden life goes on. Not just the blue-tongue, but two kinds of skink and/or gecko. I don't have the knowledge to identify these with certainty, but the brown one with the black stripe along its side may be Bougainville's skink. The other is some sort of wall lizard.

When John was a pre-schooler, we found a gecko in the yard one day, and it didn't dart away fast enough. I caught it, carefully, and put it into John's hand. He cautiously cupped his other hand over it, and it did not move. Nor did John. Then he let some light fall on it, and slowly removed the covering hand, while the gecko stayed perfectly still.

What happened next was imperceptible at first, and

when it had progressed a little it was John who noticed it. Slowly the gecko grew paler in colour, the way I had read chameleons do, as if it was trying to approximate the colour of John's hand. When we let it go, it sped away under the shelter of a row of capsicums.

I don't know if it was our imagination or not that the gecko changed colour. I don't know if we have geckos in Adelaide that do, but it was a hushed moment for both of us. John tells me he has totally forgotten it.

I see the little lizards (geckos, skinks) everywhere in the yard. When Peter Bornholm and I repaired our fence, they came out of their hiding places between the palings. I have seen them in the compost bin, where there is a perpetual supply of slaters and vinegar flies. They live in the spaces under and around piles of used bricks. At night I have seen them freeze on the wall of the front verandah as the light goes on.

One day, in the middle of a heat wave, I had to move a small white cement pot, containing a plant, to put it into deeper shade. I picked up the pot – an Arturo Comelli creation – and there, in the cramped space underneath it, among the twining white roots of some plant which had sought out the dampness that there always is under a pot plant, was a tiny gecko. We both froze for a moment, and when I moved the pot again the animal ran into the leaf litter under the feijoa tree and disappeared between the fence palings.

My Son and the Lizard

For once, I saw you stand quite still
on the thin rim of wonder, God in your hand
and no tremble at all. The ribbon life
of the lizard still, too, or it shook fear

into the autumn air, so small in fright
our eyes did not detect the pulse
or see the fret. Once its eye flicked
the unlikely paths of escape, your arm

or under your shirt, or the world's-end drop
from fingers. Mostly, terrified, still
as the death-colour of apricot bark,
the blue-grey scaled-down subterfuge

open, on your cold palm, to any fall
from the predatory sky. And then, its soft skin
played its automatic fear, and turned to tan;
perceptibly slow, the colours of your cupped hand.

The Gecko

On a day of heat I lift a pot of lavender
to carry into deeper shade. Beneath it,
alive and desperately cool, a gecko
is suddenly exposed.

His stone-damp bath of shade will bake in an hour.
The whole grey body writhes as he runs,
feet minute and frail as pinfeathers,
seeking shadow in some black depth of day.

The Athel Pine at the Desert's Edge

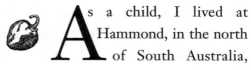s a child, I lived at Hammond, in the north of South Australia, between Wilmington and Carrieton, on the Willochra Plain. This was dry-bone country at the best of times, opened up to agriculture in the 1870s, when South Australia's government was unable to resist the pressure from people wanting to take up land. The settlers – in our part of the plain mostly Irish and German – took out most of the trees, had one or two good seasons with satisfactory crops, and then began to endure the droughts that are the norm in this part of the state.

Hammond is more or less on Goyder's line, a line of a surveyor's imagining on the map of South Australia. Beyond the line lies that part of the state in which agriculture is always going to be risky for lack of rain.

Goyder's line ran through our house, right through the middle of our dining room, so that if my mother cut flowers she had to put them on the mantelpiece. Put them on the sideboard and they withered and the water in the vase dried up. We had to put the rainwater tank at the front of the house. The house faced south, where the rains were!

Gardening was almost impossible at Hammond, because when the small dam near the cemetery ran dry, the water supply was switched to the farm mains supply from the Coonatto Creek. This permanent and reliable flow came from a spring in the creek bed in the shadow of the Horseshoe Range, a formation similar to Wilpena, but much smaller and less well known. Though it was all right for sheep, the Coonatto water was no good at all for gardens.

So it was that gardens at Hammond consisted of wormwood hedges, boxthorn hedges, agaves around which spectacular sand drifts formed, and pepper trees. Then someone discovered the athel tree (as we called it), usually known as the athel pine or tamarisk. It was hardy, had deep-reaching roots that tolerated the saline water it found when it reached the water table, grew quickly and provided good shade. Farmers began to put it in for shade and windbreaks. It prospered.

My mother planted an athel tree in the yard, for the shade. She came from the well-watered and tree-friendly hills around Crystal Brook.

The athel tree grew well. It thrived on the buckets of soapy water we gave it from the laundry, and greasy water from washing up. No one wasted water in the North.

Dad sold up in 1950 – all three tiny farms, the sheep, the shop, and the house. Our family income from all of these was very small. We moved south. I was already in school in Adelaide and my brother had to start secondary school, which was not available anywhere near Hammond. It was not a move marked by foresight, for the Korean War broke out shortly afterwards and wool prices shot through the ceiling. The few who were left in the North did well for a while.

The athel tree did well, too, for when I revisited Hammond twenty-five years later, it was still there in the yard. It was tall and had spread wide, and the ground underneath it was bare, though the rest of the yard was full of dry country weeds – thistles and roly-poly bushes. The house had been knocked down, to use the stone to build shearers' quarters, and low mounds of rubble marked where the rooms had been. At the back of the yard, along the Cormacks' fence (long gone, like the Cormacks) was the galvanised wash trough, almost untouched by the years. A lizard scuttled away when I turned it with my toe.

The home of the athel tree, *Tamarix aphylla*, and many of the sixty related species, is in the Middle East. One member of the tamarisk family produces a white sweet substance that the Bedouins eat. It is one of the many foods they call manna.

If I have seen another athel tree since 1975, I haven't consciously noted it. However, the tree is in the news, because a CSIRO scientist called Graham Griffin has drawn attention to the ecological threat posed by *Tamarix aphylla*.

The athel pine is now established in the Finke River system leading to Lake Eyre, and on some other inland waterways, where it forms very dense stands that choke out all other vegetation. Because the athel pine has no predators, and has evolved to make efficient use of the saline inland water, there is concern for the bird life that depends on Lake Eyre if it were to become established on the margins of the lake.

It is not only the dense stands of the tree which create problems. The fact that it uses all available water, and then excretes salt onto the surface of the soil through its leaves, makes it a menace. Gum trees cannot tolerate the changed soil conditions, and the loss of them means the loss of the birds, animals, and insects that depend on them.

So once again something we thought would be useful is turning against us. Hammond (population now zero, but fluctuating) has our one athel pine, and one only, unlikely to reproduce because it is a long way from the Coonatto Creek, which rarely runs and never spills over in the direction of the town on the rare occasion it is in flood.

Air Raids

Many birds come to our garden, natives and introduced species, but I have only once or twice seen magpies stalking insects on the lawn with that stately, arrogant walk that magpies have.

I can understand the magpies' arrogance, for many people have at some time been scared of them.

City pedestrians meet them in spring, in the parks, diving at them if they go too near their nests. They are aggressive and territorial during their nesting season, and many a bloodied scalp has resulted from their sharp beaks.

When I was a boy in short pants at Hammond, and was sent to fetch Dad's cows for milking, I was often attacked by nesting magpies. My defence was to carry a stick, which I kept waving above my head when I was near their trees, and usually this worked. Not always. I still recall the flurry of wings as the magpie stalled to strike after dropping down on me, the angry squawk at the last moment, the thump on the head, the pain, and then the blood seeping onto my exploring hand.

One person in our town, however, made herself immune from magpies. This was Coll, a girl who lived next door.

Coll's father was J.B., who sat all day, every day, on a stool at the corner of their home, watching the scant town traffic and puffing his pipe, which seemed never to go out. Coll's mother was Annie, a huge woman who was responsible for the disbandment of our air raid shelter digging project. When the Japanese raided Darwin, someone told us that Hammond was next because of the railway bridge outside the town; then when they took down the town name from the post office and the railway station, the town boys (all three of us) decided to save the town.

The other two boys were somewhat younger. I was the only other boy my own age in the whole town, and had been for years.

We collected our fathers' shovels and went to the sale yards, to dig the air raid shelter into which Hammond could retire when the inevitable raid came.

Stage One: discussion and planning. We would need an entrance for people to go down. That was when Annie came out to the fence to throw her dish water into the sale yards. We looked at her massive girth, thought through the problem of getting her into an air raid shelter through the entrance, gave up, and spent the next hour meanly lobbing cowpats from the sale yards into Annie's yard, trying to hit Coll.

Annie and J.B., in their slimmer and more vigorous youth, had had a large family, the youngest of whom was Coll. She was the only one still at home, and she was 'not all there'. I think she was a Down's syndrome sufferer, a woman in her twenties who spoke only in slurred sounds and had never been to school.

Coll, however, had beaten the magpies.

I remember the first day she did so. A new family of fierce nesting magpies had set up home in the gum tree in the post office yard, next door to Coll's home. They had already chased me and seen me off. Later, I heard their angry cries and the sound of their wings, and then a loud metallic clank. This was followed by extraordinary squawks from the birds, more wings, more clanks, and the magpies retired to their tree. I went outside, and there was Coll in the yard, with a look of victory on her face, and a saucepan on her head.

Whenever she went outside after that, during magpie season, Coll wore her saucepan hat. For a few days the magpies dived on her, hit (and hurt) their beaks on her saucepan, and finally learnt their lesson. From then on, nobody wearing a dress was attacked by these magpies.

Forty years later, I met a man who visited Hammond regularly, where one of his friends owned a railway cottage as a holiday shack. He told me the gum tree is still there, and the descendants of my magpie antagonists still dive viciously at anyone coming near them.

Schinus Molle and Mud Pies

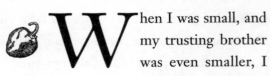

When I was small, and my trusting brother was even smaller, I fed him one day some small mud pies decorated with attractive pink berries from a tree in our yard.

This tree was a pepper tree, *Schinus molle*, with a trunk listing about fifteen degrees off vertical and therefore easy to climb. It was huge, we thought, and we played in, around, and under it a lot of the time. There was a swing on one of the branches. When I revisited the town, years after we had left, I could see that it had shrunk, in the same way that the grandparents, churches and rooms of childhood had all shrunk as I grew.

Lots of people wrongly assume that the pepper tree is an Australian native, for it can be seen in many parts of the country. The tree is commonly used as a shade tree. There is a great beauty about it, with its graceful feathery foliage and the weeping habit of its branches. It looks after itself in dry country, and is often now seen, in association with the unhappy decay of farms and small towns, as an icon of a landscape being slowly depopulated.

I have seen several country towns where the pepper tree was used for street planting, in the plantations which ran down main streets. Sometimes they have been used in the Adelaide suburbs, but because the roots get into drains, and destroy paving, they are out of favour with councils.

This tree is a South American migrant of the 19th century, which probably came via California. The commonest pepper tree is a native of Peru, and a smaller Brazilian variety is sometimes seen. It is called a pepper tree because of the clusters of red berries that the female trees bear in autumn and winter. The leaves have a pleasant pepper-like scent when crushed. The berries are not the peppercorns of the spice rack, though they are sometimes dried and ground and added to pepper. In its native continent the tree's berries are used in medicines and drinks because of their hot taste. In this country, they have possibly only ever been used in mud pies.

My neighbours have a pepper tree, 12 metres or so from the boundary fence, old and handsome. It is only in this last dry year that its scattered berries have begun to germinate in my yard. I wonder if this means that the climate is now marginally changed, to the tree's benefit?

The Bad Plant

My brother Eugene lives in the west of the city, just beyond the parklands, in a huge old corner house with plenty of room for a garden. He has green fingers, particularly with ornamentals, and grows vegetables as well.

One of the secrets of his success is that he is outgoing and gets to know the locals and picks up their lore from them. Since most of the people living around him are elderly Italians, with all the time of retirement to grow their vegetables, Eugene has been learning their tricks.

His several varieties of pickled olives, made with his own adaptations of local Italians' recipes, are extremely good.

When I last visited him, he showed me his garden, including a plant I did not recognise. It was in a pot, about 60 centimetres tall and growing fast, covered in thorns. Not only was the stem bristling with sharp thorns, but the leaves, front and back, had their own thorns jutting up at regular intervals from the veins.

'Don't touch that,' said my brother, 'or you'll be sorry.'

I didn't touch it, and he didn't know its name. He was keeping it to try to replicate something his Italian neighbours did. They kept this spiny plant, which grew quite tall, and grafted buds of aubergine plants on to its stem. In this way they had aubergines all year around. I asked him what his Italian neighbours called this plant, but they didn't have a name for it. They called it the bad plant.

I had rarely grown aubergines, but I like a challenge, and so Eugene agreed to get me a plant. He told me they had seeds like nuts, and could be grown from seeds.

At Christmas he arrived with two seedlings and a more advanced plant in a pot. These are now growing fast and dangerously at the back of the yard, brilliantly green and perilous to touch.

One day Grandpa looked at them and asked me why I had castor oil plants growing there. I had been trying to find out their name, without success. A check in a reference book, which contained an indistinct photograph, seemed to verify that they were castor oil plants.

Further reading, on the mistaken presumption that they were castor oil plants, showed why Eugene's friends might have called it the bad plant. The seeds of a castor oil plant are very dangerous. Eating three will cause death, and has done so. The seeds are crushed for their oil, but the poison is removed for medical use.

I remembered an incident many years ago. My grade one teacher at Hammond was Flexmore Hudson, the Jindyworobak poet. He and his wife had gone walking one weekend, and she had eaten castor oil plant seeds, and had nearly died. They grew wild near Hammond, as they do in many places in Australia. The plant's original home is in Africa.

However, Grandpa and I were wrong about my plant. I decided to check, and took a cutting to the Botanic Gardens. It wasn't a castor oil plant, as a *Solanum* (the aubergine) couldn't be grafted to it. After a search of the references, the officer told me that it was *Solanum hispidum*. Another officer said he had heard that some growers in Western Australia were using it to graft aubergines on to. *Solanum hispidum* is originally from tropical America, and is now naturalised in northern New South Wales.

My *Solanum hispidum* is now as high as the shed, and I lop large pieces off it regularly and put them in the garbage bin. Its thorns are quite dangerous, and persist on the leaves long after they have fallen and dried, so that weeding and cleaning up under the bush requires gloves. I have begun to try to graft aubergines onto the bush, and at present one of my three grafts has taken and there is a healthy shoot. I am content with one in three as this is the first time I have ever tried to graft.

Pecking Order

For several years my brother Brian had travelled to Melbourne some days of most weeks to work for his company, but had resisted moving there to live. Eventually, he could not put off the move any longer, and with his children all grown up the argument that their schooling might be interrupted was no longer valid. So the move was planned, and I became the solution to the problem of giving Joey a home.

Joey was their galah (*Kakatoe roseicapilla*). This pink-and-grey cockatoo had been theirs for fifteen years, since it was a baby. It lived in a large wooden cage at the end of their yard, trying to eat its way out.

Joey could not go to Melbourne, as my brother intended to rent accommodation until they found the house they wanted, and could not stay, as their house was to be rented out and my nephews and niece did not want to look after Joey. Would I be able to look after him until they returned to Adelaide?

I jumped at the chance, because I had wanted for years to have some birds, and so I bought a double aviary and installed it. While I was waiting for Joey to move, I filled one side of the aviary with zebra finches, and put a pair of quail in each side.

The finches immediately set about populating their new universe as fast as they could, and that's fast. The quail filled the nights with their mournful cries full of longing and distance. These cries carry a long way, and I imagine that's how boy quail meets girl quail in the Mallee.

Then the phone call came from my brother. 'We're definitely going. Come and get Joey. Bring a pair of gardening gloves and something to carry him in which he can't eat his way out of.'

Joey must have smelt trouble the moment I arrived, and was angry. The gardening gloves saved a lot of blood when I entered the cage and took hold of him. I could nevertheless feel his bites through them.

To transport him, I took with me a small tin trunk, as I had seen how Joey had demolished the sides of the packing case he lived in. I tied it with rope, not wanting to share my car with a distressed and biting bird.

As I left, Brian told me that Joey was a one-man bird, and had never let the children or Josie touch him. Joey the bird? Josie the wife? That's right. I'm not explaining.

At home, I got Joey into his new cage with little trouble, and he settled fairly soon. He ignored, and I imagine didn't understand, the quail on the floor. He didn't ignore the perches, and set about eating those. I replaced them with some hardened gum tree branches.

Soon he was letting me scratch him, through the

mesh, showing me that galah expression that speaks of some ecstatic tactile experience. He learnt to come to the front of the cage when he heard me leave the house, and grew to expect goodies from me – seed heads, thistles – which he enjoyed.

Eventually he let me handle him. In view of his attempts to eat me on the day I acquired him, this took courage on my part. His nibbles were friendly nudges at my fingers and ear, nothing more. He started to sit on my shoulder, and I started to carry him around the yard with me when I was working. None of this says I had won his confidence. It only says that he thought I was Brian.

When I was on my hands and knees weeding, Joey would jump off my shoulder and begin working through the soil for whatever he could find to eat. He stayed close to me, and never attempted to escape.

Pompey the cat was interested, and was driven off in a series of fierce sallies. Pompey learnt respect for Joey very early.

Joey tolerated Andrew and John, and let them scratch him when he was sitting on my arm, but that's as far as his tolerance went. Women were not wanted anywhere near him. If I was working in the garden, with Joey alongside me, and Tina or Emma appeared in the garden, to pull carrots or hang out washing or whatever, Joey left me and chased them. His intentions were fierce and mean, and were signalled with a great amount of noise. We developed an understanding that I put him away when they wanted to come outside.

So Joey seemed to have decided that this was home: friends with me because I was Brian; a *modus vivendi* with my sons just as he had with Brian's sons; and quick hostility towards women. Joey and Josie had not got on, they told me.

Who said I couldn't get him to like me?

Then, one morning, he was on the floor of the cage, looking terribly small and harmless, dead. He had been with me for six months. There had been no warning. He had looked and acted healthy.

They never really adjust to change, I was told by Josie. He would have died of a broken heart, said my sister-in-law, who made no secret of her own unhappiness at having to move to another city.

Joey was not an attractive bird, in appearance or really in personality, given his animosity towards much of the world. He began his life in a cage quite young, I am told, and maybe never learnt that he was a bird. His appearance was that scruffy look pet galahs all have, and he was a vicious biter. Galahs have never had a good press in Australia, and their name has been a favourite epithet for condemning the culpably stupid among us.

I have a favourite mental picture of galahs, in their hundreds, on the ovals at my school and in the paddocks of the neighbouring farm school, in the early light, picking at the soil for food. Their pink and grey plumage is fresh and clean, they fly and wheel with grace, but on the ground, as they waddle from place to place feeding, or stand still and watch warily, they are like funny little people. Like antipodean leprechauns.

Cocky

This cocky looks to be about the size
of a turkey drumstick, but has got
more feathers – a scrap or two, but more.

He is, she is – owners never know –
a de-feathered relic from some grassland,
passed from cage to cage. I've known

old bits and bones of early saints
with better documented provenance. O bird,
early warning system of your own back yard,

come down here where I can take a bite
of your fingers. Come. Give up hacking
at packing cases, wanting out. I think

I shall surround myself with cocky wire
of a stronger gauge, grow giant sunflowers
twelve feet tall, and let you feed and grate

your cockatoo obscenities at me. Know
that I have been asked to baby-sit you, for a mere
five years or so. Co-operation, budgie, is the word.

Love of Magnolias

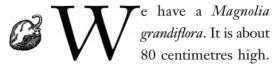**W**e have a *Magnolia grandiflora*. It is about 80 centimetres high. This is the second time it has got to this height.

It was going well, growing slowly in the front garden, when Andrew in year eleven decided to have a party. Some of his guests took their departure through the magnolia and knocked off most of the growing shoots. Only a few leaves were left for me to stand in front of and give Andrew a lecture.

The rejuvenated young magnolia still has a long way to go, and many years, for *Magnolia grandiflora* can reach 25 metres. In our lifetime we won't see anything near that.

The reason we planted it is largely nostalgia. Before we were married Tina lived in a house (just across the street from this house) that had an 8-metre magnolia. She remembers the rich citrus-tinged scent of its flowers well, and their spectacular white cups, as big as plates, which seem to glow on balmy summer evenings. We still walk past it and envy the family who now own the house.

One advantage of this tree is that it is evergreen. Most of the other magnolias are deciduous.

Magnolia grandiflora is the Southern magnolia of the

United States, and its name has resonances from all the romantic novels and movies of the Old South. It is sometimes called the bull bay, which seems to me a curious name for a sweetly scented tree, because it sounds more like the stereotype of the southern United States sheriff.

Pierre Magnol (1638–1715), for whom the magnolia is named, was director of France's oldest botanical gardens at Montpellier in southern France. The species was described from those parts of the American South that used to be the French territory of Louisiana.

Someone, some day, long after we are gone from this house, will perhaps envy the one we planted. Provided there are no more wild parties. Or this future owner will curse me for putting in the garden a tree that will eventually be too big for the space.

Olé for Chestnuts

In the front garden is the Southern magnolia, and in the back garden is a chestnut tree, both of which will grow to mythic proportions in the next couple of centuries. They may or may not survive, depending on the rise and fall of sea level, the grinding of glaciers, the ozone layer, the greenhouse effect, and so on.

It is more likely that the chestnut will fall to a bulldozer, when someone decides that several families could live where one family at present occupies one ramshackle house. However, if this doesn't happen, a future landholder, around AD 2090, will look at a tree that has spread 25 metres – wider than the block – and say: 'This thing must go'; and the Society for the Preservation of Anything Someone Else Wants to Remove will take steps to protect it.

Its most likely fate is a slow death by thirst, for a mature chestnut tree in Adelaide (a dry city where water entitlements have been sharply reduced) will need more water than the average householder is allowed.

Meanwhile, the tree has reached my height, bearing its third crop of chestnuts when it should be barren.

When we put in this tree, we planted two as the gardening guides said we should: a Flemish, prolific, and a Flemish, mahogany. The northern tree, the Flemish, prolific, died after a year; the other struggled for a while and then seemed to thrive. The two trees were needed because chestnut trees are not self-fertile. Buying one of each was an expensive business.

In the first year, three chestnuts set on the mahogany chestnut and then its neighbour died. All three fell off before ripening. In the second year, a dozen set and all ripened. In the third and fourth year, many dozens of chestnuts set, but about half fell without plumping out as they should. A heavy early autumn watering caused the rest to grow fat and ripen, and we had several splendid evenings eating roasted fresh chestnuts.

I assume that somewhere close a neighbour has a chestnut tree, but have not been able to discover where.

I think that in gardening and in cooking we spend some of our adult lives trying to recreate what we remember fondly from our childhood (hence my failed experiments to try to get a quandong to grow). Tina's childhood was spent in Clare, South Australia, home of great wines, and cool and wet enough to support a chestnut tree. She has vivid memories from her childhood of eating roasted chestnuts in winter, which was a practice her parents brought from Northern Italy where they grew up, surrounded (then, at least) by millions of chestnut trees.

When Tina describes these days in Clare, her eyes

light up as she relives the warm domestic moment of waiting for the chestnuts to roast, and then eating them, still perilously hot.

As a result it was Tina who suggested we put in a chestnut tree when the time came to fill with trees the former football patch the boys had outgrown. (There was an unexpected bonus in doing this: no one has ever been able to bring in a marquee for a party because there are trees in the way. I don't envy the people who invite a hundred guests to party under canvas on their tennis courts!)

The chestnut tree is of the same family as the oak and the beech. The most common species in Australia is the Spanish chestnut, *Castanea sativa*. This is the species that grew right across Southern Europe and Asia Minor, and grew densely around the old Greek city of Kastanaia in Asia Minor. In these places it was a tree of considerable economic importance. It produced a food crop and also a timber of reasonable quality with a reputation for endurance (imagine fence posts that last for fifty years).

Unfortunately a large part of the European population of *Castanea sativa* was destroyed by chestnut blight, particularly in Italy from 1938 onwards, just after the American population had succumbed. To date this blight has been kept out of Australia. North-east Asian producers grow a large part of the current world production, on trees of a different species.

Trivia question about chestnuts: What is the connection between yabbies, Spanish dancing, parquetry floors and chestnuts?

The word chestnut comes from the Greek *kastanéa*, and the musical instrument used to punctuate Spanish dancing, the castanet, derives from the same word. One look at a chestnut or a castanet will show the similarity of shape and colour.

Parquetry floors in grand houses used to be made of chestnut wood; imagine the frenetic click and clack of a troupe of Spanish dancers – *Olé* – with their heels pounding on a good parquetry floor and their chestnuts/castanets flying in their hands.

Marron is one of the French names for the chestnut. Coincidentally it is also the name given in Western Australia to the freshwater crayfish, which is their version of the yabby. The word in this case is from a Western Australian Aboriginal language.

I have never met a family called Chestnut, but there are plenty of Italian–Australian families called Marrone (chestnut) and Greek–Australians called Kastanos.

Something Nasty from Port Lincoln

It was originally from Portugal, but its first Australian landing was at Port Lincoln, probably via a ship's ballast or in a packing case, curled up for the duration. Maybe even silently in someone's luggage. This was in 1953. From there, this provincial pest made its way to the metropolis and settled in to Adelaide.

It's amazing how suddenly the Portuguese millipede became a crisis in Adelaide's suburbs. The loud cries came from the Adelaide Hills first, where the millipede began to appear in plague proportions, and people found their houses being invaded by them.

I remember we drove to Scott Creek to visit a friend one Sunday, and stopped at the Longwood Post Office to get our bearings from the map. The post office was surrounded by an inches-deep sea of dead millipedes.

It seemed that nothing wanted to eat them, living or dead, and all the millipedes wanted to do with their lives was to consume leaf litter and the humus in the soil, and make their way into houses to escape the cool, damp conditions outside.

The newspapers were filled with reports of ways to stop them – what kinds of poisons to use, what kinds of barriers to put up; and also complaints from people who expected the government – any government – to have a quick answer to the problem.

The Portuguese millipedes probably weren't doing much economic damage – the occasional loss of seedlings excepted – but they were nauseating people by their appearance and irritating people by their persistence. You could sweep several thousands from your doorstep one night and find that a new legion was there the next.

They may in fact have been of some economic importance to the manufacturers and salespersons in the pesticide and barrier construction industries; and eventually with government help became a focus for research by scientists.

Their numbers had grown so great in South Australia because they lacked the natural predators that kept them down in Portugal and Spain, and because the damper climate of the Adelaide Hills provided more leaf litter and humus for them to eat than their natural home. It was known that the hedgehog ate them happily in Europe, but Australia didn't want another rabbit let loose. Especially a slow one with spikes.

Australia is very cautious about importing anything and letting it loose without a carefully monitored trial, but eventually a parasitic wasp was released, which had little effect, and then a nematode, which did better.

The government interest in funding research into millipedes coincided with the march of the millipedes into the marginal electorates on the Adelaide Plains. When they arrived in my marginal back yard I kept an eye on them, and worked out ways of keeping their numbers down.

I noticed that the millipedes congregated on the white walls of the house after sundown on cool evenings at the start of autumn, and again in early spring, and I made it a habit to go outside and circle the house once every evening equipped with a torch and a long hook. This was to brush them off the walls so that I could step on them. The skin of a millipede is so tough that it cracks audibly when stepped on.

Each night there would be fewer, dropping within a fortnight from a high of 120 to a dozen or so. I no longer seem to need to hunt them, because, while the millipedes are still around, their numbers are now low. The Department of Agriculture believes that the control methods are working.

There is some anecdotal evidence suggesting that birds are starting to prey on the millipedes. I've seen the blackbirds in my garden dealing with the younger ones, and I know that quail will eat them, because when I throw millipedes to them they swallow them greedily.

Ants don't touch dead millipedes. They lie crushed on the path until they desiccate and then crumble and blow away. The ants march around them.

These many-legged creatures are of the class

Myriapoda, and there are plenty of native Australian species. These evolved here and so have their own predators here. It is only the Portuguese critter that gives trouble.

What do you do with a Portuguese millipede that finds its way inside? It will be found stationary on a wall, or wriggling its way along a carpet. If you pick it up and throw it outside into the darkness, it will be back. It will survive a fall or a toss with all the toughness of a cat.

When a Portuguese millipede is touched, it has an instant reflex action of rolling up into a coil, with all its tender parts protected. At least then it doesn't wriggle as I carry it to the toilet. When I drop it in, it sinks, still coiled, and presumably drowns.

Two Rules of Millipedes.
1. A millipede intruding on a bedroom will be seen only by someone reading in bed.

2. A millipede intruding on a bedroom can be removed only by some other person who is nearly asleep.

Lemons and Lots of Sugar

The lemon tree was dying back, and while there was a little fresh growth, the tree was sick. Urgent measures were needed.

Firstly, I bought a Lisbon lemon and planted it in a rarely used patch at the end of the yard, near to but not in danger from the incinerator. It grew quickly, and in a year put on its first fruit.

This tree has a lot of competition from a fig tree in the Rosemeads' yard. I help it along by trenching along the fence line every year or so to keep out at least the surface roots of the fig. Now, six years later, it has overflowed the space available and has to be kept in trim. It has overshadowed one garden bed and made the growing of vegetables difficult in it; and I have had to abandon going along the path on that side of the tree. In general, I like to prune the tree back and encourage it to put on height so that I can walk under it.

My father-in-law, on the other hand, adopts a different and covert method he has used for years. From time to time I discover, in the leafy depths of the tree, a series of bracing ropes engineered so that the tree works against itself and keeps the offending branches hoisted up out of the way.

Grandpa said to me once, when I got upset about

some unnecessary pruning of a tree to make it easier for him to walk along a path instead of choosing another a few metres away: 'I'm not going to get out of the way of a tree!'

This new tree gives us a copious supply of lemons, with plenty to give away. The dying tree has taken on a second life, because as soon as the new tree was established I gave the older tree a haircut, and pruned back every branch to head height.

One of the signs of the intelligence of trees is the way that some trees get the message. This tree, after the haircut, put on new growth everywhere, and is now vigorous, healthy, and bigger than it was before.

Another lemon tree I used to see daily, across the fence in the Bornholms', failed to get the message that dying branches were out of favour. My neighbour never took off the dead wood, and let mistletoe take over, and eventually all but one small section of the tree was dead.

The lemon tree is *Citrus limon*, the name coming from Persian and Arabic *limun*, which was originally used for all citrus fruits. The tree was described in Arabic writings of the 12th century, and possible remains of lemons have recently been found in the ruins of Pompeii.

This discovery, if verified, confronts the conventional wisdom that the Greeks and Romans did not know the lemon. Some time after AD 1000 the fruit was introduced into North Africa and Europe, and the Crusaders made the fruit popular after their return home.

Champion lemons have been grown that weigh up to 1.8 kilograms. An American (presumably without tastebuds) ate three whole lemons (sliced into quarters) in 15.3 seconds in a crazy contest in 1979. This included the skins and the pips.

What he went through as a taste thrill can be judged by Mrs S. P. Bond's recipe in my old *Green and Gold Cookery Book*. Mrs Bond's lemon marmalade recipe uses a pound (454 grams) of sugar to each thinly cut lemon. A large lemon from my tree weighs only half a pound.

The fruit is called *Zitrone* in German, *limón* in Spanish, *limone* in Italian, and *limão* in Portuguese. The French call the lemon *citron*. I wonder what they call a car that is a lemon!

The French certainly knew about their lemons. King Louis XIV decorated the Hall of Mirrors at Versailles with lemon trees planted in tubs of solid silver. Two Louis later, when the French decided that their kings were lemons, the silver tubs were melted down, and we all know that the king was pruned at shoulder height.

Cheap Mulch

The Electricity Trust of South Australia keeps a careful eye on its power lines, and regularly sends a team down the street to prune any branches that look as if they are going to pose a danger to them. The team is first seen as a couple of leaders, who suss out the territory, reassure the householders, explain the rationale of what they are doing, and decide where the trees (in street or garden) need to be pruned. Though their mandate presumably stops at the fence line, there is an obligation on residents to keep trees away from the lines that cross gardens to go to the house, and the ETSA teams sometimes help by pruning these trees back too, with the householder's consent.

Further down the street will be heard the sounds from the next members of the team, high on a cherry-picker with a saw, pruning and dropping. They are followed by an even louder noise, created by a machine that sucks in the branches thrust into it and turns them into a spray of chips and leaf litter.

Usually a friendly gardener can get the ETSA workmen to hand over a load of these chips for mulch, and I imagine that they are glad to do so. Let me speculate: it probably saves them money, because they do not have the expense of transporting the chips to a dump somewhere; and the kind of gardener who values the chips as mulch is also the kind of gardener who will take pen to paper and complain of the vandalism (as he sees it) being inflicted on trees when for a few hundred million dollars the whole electricity supply system could be undergrounded. Thus a local public relations plus may avoid a wider loss through the letters to the editor.

One fine day, when the ETSA team were working in our street, my father-in-law Giovanni asked me casually if I minded if he asked them for some of the mulch.

'Go ahead,' I said. 'Get as much as they'll give you.'

Then I left to go to work. That night I parked my car on the road; I couldn't get it in the drive. We barrowed and barrowed and barrowed until dark, and could by then see that we had made some small impact on the pile. There's a certain difficulty, which I discovered that night, about driving a shovel into a mound of wood chips and expecting to get far.

We had so much free mulch that we quickly ran out of places to put it, and began to dump second and then third loads in some places until it was running over the edges of beds and onto paths. There was a pile around every fruit tree; and then we created paths of this chippy mulch through the vegetable garden. We left mounds of it along the undeveloped sides of the yard, and mounds of it at the end of the yard. We had far too much.

Grandpa would have been a good haggler in a bazaar – he's a persistent man – but I don't know what really went on in his negotiations with ETSA to lead to the super-abundant generosity with mulch which then plagued me for several years.

Leaf litter is excellent mulch and becomes excellent compost; throw a few spadefuls of dirt over it and the small things get to work and integrate it into the growth of the garden in no time at all. When you watch ETSA working, what you see is great leafy boughs being pushed into their machine; what you don't stop to think about is the fact that the overwhelming proportion of what comes out, by weight and by volume, is chunks and lumps of wood, thumb-sized, half thumb-sized, which dry out completely in a few weeks and then take several years to rot down into the soil.

Fortunately, as my mountains of mulch dried out, and in particular as the leafy component dried, shrank, and rotted, the sheer volume was less of an embarrassment and was able to be contained, was able to be raked back off the paths it was spilling on to, was able to be kept from overwhelming beds of vegetables. Yes, it kept down weeds, there is no doubt of that, and provided a multitude of foraging grounds for slaters, but the fact is that I still had a random collection of pieces of wood, unreconstructed and unrepentant, in the soil and around shrubs, for several years. And every cedar berry that was in it germinated and had to be removed. The pieces took on the appearance of bones (since I recycle everything, I have many chicken bones throughout my garden). Some parts of the garden I cleaned up with a rake, removing many of the largest pieces to the incinerator for their final damnation.

Never again, I said, never again. My own garden generates better mulch and compost.

A Million Ways with Compost

In the year of my conversion to composting, I had mounds of plant material scattered around the yard – weeds, kitchen peelings, dead leaves and flowers, and so on. I made sure to mix plenty of soil with them, in layers, and to turn them regularly. They were popular with slaters and earthworms and other small life I don't have names for, and in a matter of weeks the plant material was broken down and the resultant rich humus was able to be spread into the garden beds.

An alternative to the mound was to create an airy container from a piece of wire netting, shape it into a cylinder and fill it with the same kinds of material, plant waste and soil, in layers. This works, but it is certainly slower, and has the disadvantage that it cannot be turned to aerate it. Besides, I found the structures to be fairly ugly.

What to do with kitchen waste under this regime – bones and meat scraps, chicken carcasses, egg shells, cups of fat, crusts of bread and leftover custards? (I remember our first home, in a bare little flat, facing the choice of wrapping a mouldy custard tart to put it into the garbage bin, or mixing it with so much water that it could be washed down the sink.) My strategy for dealing with these once I owned a suburban block was to bury them. Some people I know use a trench, and fill it in through the week. I prefer the one-off hole, covering the waste straightaway. This makes it necessary to wait for a couple of weeks before planting seedlings or sowing seeds on a patch that has been used this way, because as the waste decays it reduces in volume and the soil sinks. There's also another problem, and this problem is four-footed.

That's the wandering neighbourhood cat and dog. Either of these will happily dig up a recently buried bucket full of scraps for the trimmings off the T-bone or the chicken giblets, leaving a mess for you to clean up next day. I worked out a couple of simple ways to deal with this problem. One is the mobile brick, not lofted into the air after the scratching bitzer, but placed on the surface over the most recently buried scraps and left there for a few days. I've not had any problems since I started doing this. A similar solution, and just as effective, is to cover up the buried scraps and then drive the spade firmly down immediately above the sweet-smelling trove. Dogs and cats can't cope with that either. If it rains heavily, and the spade falls sideways as the soil gets soft, the cats and dogs are still deterred because they don't like to dig in rain-sodden earth either.

My father-in-law is a kind of lost Leonardo da Vinci – he can invent an ingenious solution to almost any problem, using the world-record collection of bits and pieces he keeps in his shed (it is sometimes called our shed and almost never my shed). I imagine that he analysed the problem something like this:

1.   Kitchen waste has to be kept from cats and dogs.

2.   It ought to be able to be used where it is needed after it has rotted, not buried some place just because the space is empty.

3.   There has to be a way of dealing with it in late spring when every inch of ground is devoted to vegetables and there is no space to dig holes.

So he built me a compost bin. It is made of brick, rendered in cement, and is about 1.5 metres long by 60 centimetres wide by 80 centimetres deep. It is in an inconspicuous place where nothing will grow because the neighbour's fig tree is just on the other side of the fence. It has a hinged lid, cut down from a Plume petroleum sign, to the scandal of the fig-tree neighbour who knew what it would bring on the curio market. At the bottom of the compost bin is a hole through which I can drag out already processed compost. It is a gem of an idea.

The heat generated inside it helps the breaking down

of plant and animal rubbish, destroys seeds, and attracts mice. I've found them nesting in it and they have joined the compost. When the attentions of mice are evident, I leave the lid open for a day and a night and a local cat deals with them. I bought a milk carton full of tiger worms and seeded this compost bin and several of my heaps with them, and they have never stopped working. It can deal with cardboard, when we have an excess of cartons, and with newspaper in small quantities. Throwing spadesful of dirt on top of kitchen waste keeps the flies away and starts the process working. It can take whole trellises of exhausted beans, bucketsful of weeds, anything except lawn clippings. Through time is a few weeks.

At around age seventy-five my father-in-law was told by his last employer that he really had to stop coming to work, and so he had all day, every day, to work in the yard and around the house. This was when he invented a task he then did almost daily, provided I kept the makings up to him. I think it began when he noticed that I used to use the blade of a spade to chop the sweet corn stems into manageable bits before composting them; so he created a chopping block, of a height that was ergonomically right, sharpened up a tomahawk and made another one from a piece of steel, and began the business of chopping up the rubbish. It's a superior way of dealing with the prunings of woody plants like broom or viburnum. The wheelbarrow sat at the end of the yard, the prunings were put in it by Tina and me, and each morning he chopped them up. Then we used them as mulch, or composted them further in a heap with some soil.

Unfortunately, if he disapproves of some of my profligate throwing away, such as a bed of radishes that have got too woody to use, he will rescue the roots and cook the best of them for himself, for his diet is a wonder to think about but not an object of beauty to observe. (He mostly cooks for himself, because this gets the timing, the flavour, the combinations and the fads just right.)

In his ninety-second year he was finding his daily task of chopping harder to do, and I bought a mechanical mulcher which handles the heavier prunings.

I have one more way of dealing with plant litter that is very effective: each year I grow a large patch of sweet corn and two or three rows of tomatoes. I plant the tomatoes on long parallel raised hills with a trench in between them, and the sweet corn in short rows. Both of these benefit from having plenty of mulch around their roots, the cost of watering is kept down, and the growth of weeds is almost entirely eliminated. So I put deep layers of plant litter in between the plants, and through the growing season the little critters in the litter dig the nutrients into the soil. When I finally finish a patch of sweet corn, say, what is left of the litter I rake up and mound and let the happy process continue while the patch rests. My sweet corn thrives, my tomatoes are prolific.

There are three things I don't add to the stream of compost – spent tomato bushes, kikuyu and couch grass. Kikuyu and couch are unkillable, grow from the tiniest scraps, and take over anywhere. I didn't have kikuyu until it came from my neighbour's. I'll never get it out of the lawn, and I wage a regular fight to stop it from invading the vegetable garden. The new path to the shed is 90 centimetres wide, a concrete path, and within six months of its being laid kikuyu had already made its way under that in two places. It will be an everlasting battle.

There is a busy magic in the recycling of plant and animal materials through composting and into the humus necessary for new growth. There are a myriad of small creatures, many of them too small to be seen with the naked eye, which do this work and gain their own profit from it, in the form of sustenance and shelter. Look under a fallen leaf.

Encyclopaedia
of life, under a dead leaf,
jumps, hurries, digs deep.

The Quail

He has assurance about him,
waits there in patience;
old generations work him
as watcher. Behind the bramble
he waits.

Three weeks he waits.

This is the patience that sees
new generations through. Watch,
and protect. Protect, and wait.

She has patience about her,
sits with assurance, warm
on the eggs. She cannot do
other than this: wait,
and wait, sit while the watcher
watches, and waits.

Three weeks warm she must sit.

Then, it is done. Four chicks
out, and hen and cock
sharing the brood, in the way
that generations insist. They squat,
wings warm, over their chicks.

In a week, the chicks race out
on seed and insect messages
of their own. The waiters
hover and bother and scratch.

Somewhere in this poem about the patience of the quail
are some of my feelings about the experience of waiting
for an expected baby, helpless to do anything except
wait – and rub my back please, John.

Raising quail ought to be easy, but somehow it isn't.
The hen seems to be very fickle, lays huge numbers of
eggs she doesn't bother to gather together as a clutch to
sit on, and then, when she decides to do so, often leaves
the clutch after a couple of weeks. Sometimes my quail
hens have brought their eggs to hatching and left the
nest when two or three of the chicks are out, leaving
several eggs with live chicks in them to go cold and die.

I suppose they know what they are doing.

What they are doing is, I imagine, adhering to
patterns imposed by thousands of generations of living in
the Mallee. Even though the hen is there in the cage with

him, the male will night after night let loose his haunting melancholy calls designed to bring a hen to him. These carry the length of several suburban back yards, and are drawn-out and full of anguish.

When (and if) the hen decides to sit on some eggs, she half-covers herself with leaf litter, grass and so forth. Added to her dull colours of the earth, she is well camouflaged.

When the chicks hatch, they are capable of running around and feeding themselves at once, though they spend a lot of time huddled under the outspread wings of the parents. Both mother and father are actively involved in their raising. It is obviously a survival mechanism for a ground-living bird to be able to run around and feed independently from the time of hatching.

For the first couple of weeks I give the baby quail some lightly scrambled egg with the addition of bran or wheat germ every second day. They love this and it seems to speed their growth. I also go to the compost heap and collect a mass of slaters in a couple of scoops of compost and throw them into the cage. The quail eat the slaters, and the slaters race frantically to hide under the leaf litter and stones in the cage. The finches fly down to the floor and have their own feast on the smaller life contained in the dirt with the slaters.

If I can catch a cricket, I throw this to the quail as well. They attack it vigorously, peck at it until they cripple it, while the cricket tries to escape, and eventually eat it. They deliberately encourage their young to join in when they are chasing insects.

Over the years I have had quail, I have noticed that in some summers the quail do not breed until autumn approaches. These years are the parching drought years. In the wild, young quail chicks would be hard put to survive, and the hens must wait until the turn in the weather indicates that grass and seeds and insects are likely to be available. A colleague at work, whose holiday recreations include quail shooting, tells me that in the same seasons quail in the wild are very scarce.

Melancholy Season

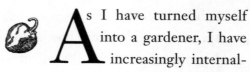As I have turned myself into a gardener, I have increasingly internalised the flow of the seasons, and I sometimes feel a sense of sadness as the end of summer comes.

So much in the garden is coming to an end. The tomatoes are past their best, the marrows and melons are finishing, the main crop of beans has stopped producing, the lettuces cook in the sun, and herbs are running to seed.

At the same time, this is my busiest time at work, which means that I am pushing uphill to find time to spend in the garden, yet the maintenance tasks and the cleaning-up cry out to be done. For a while, the watering takes priority. Other things wait.

As the days shorten, we react – physically, perhaps, or psychologically – to the transition; and in the garden I think of what seeds to sow to have food crops through the winter. More lettuce, for sure, even though it will grow slowly; leaf greens; broccoli and cauliflowers in some years. But a lot of the garden will be left to rest.

This is the season which, more than any, has urged me to write about my feelings at the change of the year and show them reflected in the miniature world of my garden.

The Beans

The beans are done. They are making me
a speech about mortality, gone brown
as crusts, alive with white fly swarms
that suck leaves dry. At the top
of the trellis, all the new shoots
live for the sun and the bees, and set
young beans that grow in a day or two
and I can barely reach. It is below,
in the litter of dust that was leaf,
that summer's end is racing up the vine.

Officially Autumn

The wind last night bent down one frond
from that banana plant that grows
next door. I tore it loose and left it
for the compost heap. I have not seen
my neighbour now for several days;
his bedroom light is early on
each night. I'm told it is his back
that's keeping him in bed. I see
my basil bushes stretching to the bees;
some, already brown and set with seed,
promise random seedlings all next spring.
I will pluck ripe basil soon
and hang it under drying eaves
for winter use. The heat is gone,
the clocks are back one hour again,
a batch of family birthdays comes
in a week or so. Autumn is here,
tired autumn, backache and bones
and settle and set and last of things.

Autumn

Someone has left a hank of rope
thrown on the bench, beside the nails.

The pruning shears are soiled
with the familiar green
of my tomato plants.

I hold my breath when I pick
the beans, which every day succumb
to the white fly. I brush the clouds
of flies away, I spray water
and cannot win. The beans become
a couple of scanty meals; no more.

Most of the lettuces are gone.
The rest are racing to seed, and slugs
at night chop and leave their slime.

Someone has left three empty pots
on the garden seat, beside the rake.

The Old Tomatoes

Today has just that still feel
of an end-of-the-season day.
I shall not water: promise
of first certain rains has come.
The tomatoes are useless now,
the fruit scarred and burnt by sun,
burrowed into, split wide open,
starting to rot. And brown blight
creeps up every plant. It's time
to pull them out. They may lie
in an empty patch until they die.

Then I shall burn, turning disease
into neighbourhood smoke. My hands
today are bright with green of sap
and crushed leaves. The tall plants
are low, and laid on a bed.

I am ready to move right on
into another good season of sun.
These wrecks of discarded plants
have served. I shall go on
to pruning, cut back tarragon
and mint, tackle the grape vine
last of all, chop it for compost
and mulch. Then dig and rake
until my aching back forces me in.

At the end of the yard, thump
and slap, ball on wall, my lad
leaps and smashes pellet-sound
tennis across the still garden
where old tomatoes lie in piles
and my back aches as I dig and rake.

Cleaning Up

This is the time for taking strawberries out.
Three years is certainly past prime

and the fruit has a cold green blight
we cannot eat. The spots of rust

on every leaf are signal enough.
The prognosis is not good.

So I must dig them out, to dry
here on the path, and then burn

the flowering disease, renew the soil,
and plant again in another place.

Part Three

Nineteen Things I Have Learnt About Carrots

1. Carrots can be transplanted but the result is ludicrous. Nature has designed the carrot to drive its root down straight into the soil. In my naive first season as a home gardener I decided to transplant some, to lay them out in neat rows; but the thin roots were impossible to replant with the straightness nature intended, and the product was carrots in curls and bows, spirals and J-curves, S-bends and pigtails. They were real enough carrots, edible, but impossible to prepare for cooking and impossible to clean for eating raw.

2. Carrots do not take well to being planted in soil which has had fresh organic matter dug into it. The roots bifurcate and even, if there is such a word, trifurcate. When the descending root meets a piece of organic matter, it splits. The cook does not enjoy preparing such carrots, even though the mass of vegetable is no less than with good carrots.

3. No matter how thinly I spread carrot seeds in the patch, I do not spread them thinly enough. I have this on the authority of two experts, my father and my father-in-law.

4. Carrots must be sown in soil worked to a fine tilth, which immediately forms a crust through which the carrots will have difficulty breaking. Some experts recommend a scattering of radish seeds, which will germinate first and break the crust.

5. The bed where the seed is sown must be kept moist to assist the young carrots to break through the soil. This is almost impossible to do when I am working, and a resident in-law is a very helpful aid. If it gets too hot in late October and early November, two or three sprinklings a day may be needed. However, I have found a remedy. After I have sown the seeds, I then lightly cover the bed with a layer of freshly cut plant material such as grape vine or bougainvillea, in sufficient quantity so that light and air get to the surface of the bed, and sunshine filters through to warm the soil. The surface does not dry out, for most of it is in shade for several parts of the day as the sun moves overhead. Using this method, I have germinated carrot seeds (and some other vegetables such as beetroot and lettuce) even in quite hot weather. However, as soon as the tiny carrots shove through the soil, the covering needs to be removed, or they quickly lose their strength in trying to put on enough height to reach the sunshine.

6. Most people have noticed that the carrot near the edge of the bed is the biggest, the best, and the earliest. For some reason carrots respond really well to a heavy tamping down of the soil, and at the edges of beds, where careless people are likely to walk on the soil, they have conditions they like.

7. The carrots Tina thinks are too small to worry about, and hence throws on the compost, are the same size as the carrots I think are a good size to eat.

8. A man wearing trifocals has a great deal of trouble seeing whether his carrots have germinated unless his knees and his back are in good shape.

9. Every weed in the garden grows faster than carrots. When the seedlings are young, the weeds begin to germinate. I have been tempted to try to get the weeds out early, but this seems to cause me to lose too many seedlings. I find it better to wait until the weeds are big enough to grasp between finger and thumb without risking the carrot.

10. Carrots turned into carrot juice in the vitamiser are one of the healthiest forms of misery known to society. The thought of alcohol made by fermenting the root flesh of carrots is a thought I prefer not to entertain.

11. It is possible to grow carrots successfully, and to eat them almost every day of the year, and still not like them.

12. A series of plantings in a large garden will give a family carrots nearly every week of the year (my best has been a gap of only six weeks), but the later patches never grow to a good size, and the last crops are always attacked by small grubs which eat into the tops and denude the carrots. Yes, I could spray and get rid of them, but I refuse to use sprays in my part of the garden. Once we decided to try to save the carrots for winter by freezing them, but no one particularly liked frozen carrots, we discovered. On another occasion we cooked and pulped a large surplus and froze it in margarine containers; it was an excellent, if rather saffron-coloured, addition to give body to the winter soups. The plastic containers were stained by the chemicals that give the carrots their colour, and could not be cleaned.

13. Ants love carrot seeds. My recipe for dealing with these involved kerosene. I mixed the seeds into a measure of sand, and then dampened it lightly with kerosene and stirred it, before sprinkling the sandy mixture in the seed bed. This deterred the ants, and did not seem to affect the germination rate. However, I noticed in years I used this trick that the number of carrots that were whitish rather than yellow or orange increased from the usual one or two per bed to a dozen or more. Using the sand, without kerosene, is also a handy way of sowing more thinly. A Vegemite jar, with nail holes in the lid, filled with sand mixed with carrot seeds and used like a pepper shaker, also makes it easier to control the sowing.

14. Once the leaves of carrots grow long enough, they provide a damp shade. The garden cat finds this a comfortable place to spend the heat of the day, with an eye open for an unwary bird. Often the first sign that the carrot patch has been adopted by the cat comes when you turn the hose onto the carrots. That black streak is the cat.

15. Carrots as they grow are able to twist around, and in their slow writhing encompass chicken bones, nails, pebbles, shells, pieces of wire and any other garbage that has found its way into the garden over the decades. I have seen a carrot that had dived through the discarded ring-pull top of a beer can and when harvested looked like an unhappy, half-completed, botched circumcision.

16. Carrots originated in or near Afghanistan and were cultivated around the Mediterranean 2,000 years ago. Flemish immigrants brought them to Britain during the reign of Elizabeth I.

17. Only the purple aubergine and the brown or red onion come to mind as vegetables that appear commonly in still life paintings. I have only once seen carrots in a painting, not a still life, and this was in *The Banquet of the Starved* by the Belgian painter James Ensor. This painting is a reflection of the sufferings of Belgium under German occupation in the First World War, which Ensor knew at first hand. The diners, who are all grotesque caricatures, are arranged like the guests and host in da Vinci's *Last Supper*. On the table, ready for the diners, are some insects, an onion, some ugly dried fish, and, as centrepiece, on a green plate, is a double-rooted, uncooked and shrivelled carrot.

18. Athenaeus, a second century Egyptian Greek, who wrote fifteen volumes called *The Gastronomers*, quoted an opinion that the carrot was an aphrodisiac. This may be connected to the custom of ladies in the court of Charles I of England. These beauties wore carrot leaves, which are undoubtedly graceful foliage, as personal adornment. What they did with the carrots themselves has not been recorded.

19. There is nothing new about carrot cake. Grated carrot was often included in old recipes for Christmas puddings, to help keep them moist. Carrot pies and puddings were out of favour for a time, but returned to the menu during the hardships and sugar shortages of the Second World War. Stretching 300 grams of mincemeat to make rissoles for a tribe is helped by the generous use of grated carrot.

A Minuet with Lettuce

I grew up in a world almost without lettuce.

My father used to buy vegetables for his small shop at Hammond from Silbert Sharp and Bishop in Adelaide, and these were sent to us on the train, which took a day to get to Hammond. No one could grow vegetables on the Willochra Plain, because the air boiled in summer, and when the reservoir dried up we were switched to the saline Coonatto spring water.

Occasionally there was a lettuce in the box of vegetables ordered from Adelaide, probably a Great Lakes lettuce. From this distance I can only speculate on its quality, several days from the farm which grew it.

My mother cut the pale lettuce hearts into fine threads. We ate this without dressing; occasionally with a tangy egg and vinegar mayonnaise. I never saw her with any other sort of lettuce. I never saw a simple oil and vinegar dressing.

At boarding school, and in the houses where I boarded when I taught in country schools, there was the same lettuce. Did anything else exist in the world?

It certainly did. Bright green bitter Italian lettuce, Cos lettuce, red chicory with creamy white leaves hidden in the heart, chicories of a variety of combinations of red and pink and green and cream, long-leaved chicories, red and brown mignonette, Roma Rosso red Cos, frilly Prizehead red, oak-leaf lettuce, rocket, and many more.

Little by little I discovered all of these, and grew many of them.

I started to meet these lettuces when I went to eat with my future in-laws, and in the homes of Tina's Italian relations. These new lettuces were torn into pieces as often as cut, and were served with oil and vinegar, and sometimes had herbs thrown in. Tina's parents were particularly fond of a bitter green lettuce they called lidric, which I think is the Friuli dialect form of the Italian *lattuga* (Latin *lactuca*). I found this hard to eat, even when I was told how healthy it was.

It was in fact a chicory, and it has made itself at home in the yard of this house. At the end of the season several plants are left to go to seed, and the seeds scatter around the dying plant and come up again at all times of the year, but mostly in spring. They also come up in hundreds whenever there is a late summer rain.

Sometimes I have simply pulled up the fully grown plant – a chicory running to seed can get to 2 metres tall – and wander around the garden hitting the seed heads on posts and stakes, so that the seeds fall. Even though we rarely eat it now, except mixed in with sweeter lettuces, we still find lidric in the yard.

For other lettuces where I want to keep the seed, it is

enough to put a plastic bag around the seed heads and hang the whole plant upside down in a dry place until the seeds fall into it.

The wide acceptance of new kinds of salad vegetables, and their availability everywhere, is almost a symbol of the way in which large immigrant groups from the 1960s have been accommodated by Australia and have in the process changed the definition of Australia.

The lettuce/chicory family grew all around the Mediterranean, and lettuces were taken to Britain by the Romans. Many of the varieties grown in Adelaide now were brought here as seeds by migrants in the last forty years, unofficially. Today, many seed companies have the new varieties available; in Vari's Italian grocery on Norwood Parade, each year there is a collection of Italian lettuce and chicory seeds for sale.

The ancient Greeks had festivals called *Adonia*, to recall the death of Adonis, after the harvest was in. Among all of the other products of the land, they carried lettuces in pots in procession, as offerings to their gods. If greenies wanted a mythical patron, they couldn't do better than Adonis, who was an agricultural divinity of both the Phoenicians and the Greeks. When he was killed by a boar, his lover Aphrodite laid him, in the funeral sense of the word, on a bed of lettuce. Moreover, and this is perhaps his best qualification as a patron of the green movement, his mother was a tree.

The pots of lettuce in the Adonis procession were accompanied by pots of other quick-to-germinate and short-lived plants, symbolising the sadness of his short life. I have never actually grown lettuces in pots, but people who live in flats and units do. Sometimes they come up in ones and twos around Tina's pot plants when she has put fresh compost into them.

I have found lettuce so easy to grow that we have our own home-grown salads nearly every day of the year, unless there has been an unusual rain, such as the summer rain which one year fell warm and persistently for five days and rotted every grown lettuce at the heart.

I sow lettuce or chicory seeds every few weeks, usually mixing several varieties. In the hottest weather, I put the seeds in the refrigerator for a couple of days before planting. This is supposed to fool the seeds into thinking that winter has passed and spring has come again.

The deception won't last if the seed is then allowed to bake hard in the soil. In really hot weather there is no point in sowing the seed, unless the surface is covered with prunings of vines or something similar to provide a shady microclimate until the seeds germinate.

It has always been a great boon to have Grandpa around the house to keep the seedlings damp while they are very small, as one watering a day in heat-wave weather won't do.

However, I have had to break him of a habit of

watering mature lettuces from overhead in hot weather, because this puts water into the hearts. As soon as the sun hits them they begin to cook and a sort of slimy soup results, which has to be thrown into the compost.

I always grow far too many lettuces, and have to thin them out, which I hate doing. Lettuce can be transplanted, but not in hot weather, for they are set back a long way by transplantation. The lettuce I do transplant as a matter of course are the lettuces that spring up randomly in the garden where seeds have been spilt or thrown. There are usually plenty of these.

Lettuce grows fast and well in a bed filled with dug-in compost and partly rotted mulch.

An old saying claims that 'If lettuce be eaten after dinner, it cures drunkenness'. I wonder if it affects the reading of a random breath test. If the crystals turn green, you've been over-indulging on lettuce!

Alexander Pope wrote a couplet recommending a method of getting a good night's sleep:

If your wish be rest,
Lettuce and cowslip wine, probatum est.

The folk wisdom that Pope drew upon for this verse is backed by modern science, which says that chemicals in lettuce leaves are tranquillisers.

If you don't like to eat your lettuce, or use it as a

soporific, try smoking it. In some places the leaves are cured in the same way as tobacco, and then smoked.

I have tried most of the lettuces and chicories offered in the seed catalogues I get, and there seem to be new varieties available quite often. I love seeing the great range of lettuce available at the markets and in good greengrocers now.

Some samples of the diversity of lettuces and chicory of Italian origin now sold in Australia are:

Cicoria variegata di Castelfranco
Cicoria zuccherina di Trieste
Cicoria bionda Triestina
Cicoria rossa di Verona a palla
Cicoria Catalogna Brindisina
Cicoria spadona da taglio
Cicoria verde a grumolo
Cicoria variegata di Chioggia
Cicoria rossa di Treviso

These, and the many others now available, seem to be quite easy to grow. Many of their names refer to the towns and villages where the variety has been treasured for centuries. I hope that the suppliers to niche markets, such as the Sant'Agata seed company, will be able to keep this diversity flourishing in the face of the market-driven push to have fewer and fewer varieties available.

I smile when I see *minuet* lettuce on sale. I think there might be a place in the employment market for a spelling consultant. I'd start with the greengrocers who can't spell *mignonette*, and then move in on that fifty per cent of all signwriters who can't spell *accommodation*.

Recently, on King William Road, Hyde Park, an upmarket shopping and out-to-lunch boulevarde, I saw a display of beautiful fresh lettuces, at a good price, and my old familiar mignonette among them. Its label proclaimed it to be *Ming* lettuce. Chinese vegetables yet!

Italian Lettuce

Someone's sister turned smuggler,
toe of a shoe to do the job,
after the holiday back home.

The lettuce seed was childhood
calling to her, nostalgia
from the mountain town.
Across the suburbs, brother to uncle,
to uncle's cousin, his friend,
the man from the next town,
the seeds and the seedlings spread.

It has been naturalised now,
like gnocchi, tomato paste,
pasta and pizza
and back yard wine.

If good rains come
in early summer, I expect
a bursting of leaves,
a pepper of green
all over my garden.
A week or two
and we gather a salad
on summer nights.

It's bitter and crisp
(but I'm used to it now)
and its names change
from house to house.

I like that uninhibited green
that forces the light
across my stretch of yard.

Glut of Tomatoes

As a topic of conversation, the tomato rivals the weather. How often do you find yourself discussing with a casual acquaintance whether or not it has been a good season for tomatoes? And how very often it has been a bad season for the person you are talking to!

I don't do anything right with tomatoes. I don't plant them at the right time by the moon; I don't prune them heavily enough; I plant them too close together; and I won't spray them no matter what happens.

That, I tell my critics, is why I can only fill the freezer with frozen tomatoes every year, eat tomatoes every day in summer and autumn, feed the relatives, and still have some left over for Tina and me to take to work and give to friends.

Usually I buy tomato seedlings, finding it a drag to raise my own. When I have dried my own tomato seeds and kept them over winter, and then sown them, they have been very slow to start and very fragile. The seedlings from the nursery have a head start and have been looked after better than I can manage. Later in spring and early summer I might pick up some of the seedling plants which have come up in the garden and transplant them to my beds, or just leave them in the corners where they come up and see what happens.

Some of my rules for preparing for a tomato crop are:

1. Use a new patch every year. This avoids any diseases left in the soil by last year's tomatoes.

2. Enrich the beds with plenty of dug-in compost about three weeks before buying the seedlings.

3. Prepare the beds as two long parallel mounds for ease of watering and of picking.

4. Put in the stakes when the beds are prepared.

5. Plant a root of tansy every metre or so along the channel between the mounds. Tansy is anathema to many of the insects that attack tomatoes.

I water seedlings daily until they are established, and as soon as the first fruits begin to set I water the plants heavily once a week. Unless the channels between the rows are clogged with mulch, this can be by flooding from one end. A jar or a tin, or a garden pot, placed over the end of the hose and weighted, cuts the force of the water coming from the nozzle and prevents it from undercutting the soil in the rows.

This regime has never been understood by my father-in-law, who waters everything he grows every day. I've failed to convert him to my system. He's failed to convert me to his.

A windy spring night can damage young tomatoes, and so I tie them up as soon as they get to about 20 centimetres in height. I trained Tina and Emma to keep old pantihose in a bag in the laundry cupboard. Since Emma left home there has been a shortage at times. Pantihose are ideal because they are so stretchable. About seven ties can be cut from one pair. They don't cut into the stems of the tomato.

As I tie the tomatoes up, I prune them, otherwise the bush goes everywhere. Towards the end of the season they grow so fast I cannot keep up with pruning them, and the last fast-growing tips straggle and loop around the bush.

There is a tremendous weight of plant and fruit, and quite often the whole plant slowly sags, the main stem loops and sits on the ground, and the bottom tomatoes hide in the mass of foliage close to the soil.

I did find a remedy for this. For a few seasons I hammered nails into the stakes before I put them in, and then when the tomatoes got heavy I tied them with the usual pantihose in a few places and hitched the pantihose ties over the nails. This worked all right if I got in first. If I tried to pull up a plant that had already slumped I inevitably broke a main stem which had already settled into a comfortable shape.

I believe that an exhausted tomato plant must not be composted. At the end of the season I pull up the stake, through the top of the plant, and then pull out the tomato, pantihose and all. I used to leave the plants to dry at the end of the yard, and then burn them, because all tomatoes have diseases at the end of the season and it makes sense not to let these continue to the next year. Now it goes into the garbage, for the large wheeled bins have been introduced by our council, and incinerators have been banned.

I have a rule I am quite ruthless about: if a young tomato plant shows signs of disease, I don't persevere with it. Into the bin it goes.

Success and failure: there's a lot of the peasant in me, and faced with a big crop of tomatoes I have no intention of letting them go to waste. Some of my methods have failed. Like the year we turned lots of tomatoes into puree, cooked and bottled it, covered it in a layer of oil, stored it in the cubby-house, and watched bottle after bottle ferment. There was more success when we turned the puree into containers and froze it.

There is a machine in the top of the cupboard which we can use to make tomato puree. It is an ingenious, hand-worked Italian machine called a *spremipomodoro* which is Italian for 'squeeze the shit out of tomatoes'. It originally belonged to Tina's mother. Cooked tomatoes and basil are put into the working end, the handle is turned, and all the seeds and skins, and the basil leaves and stalks, are separated from the pulp.

The freezer handbook advised preparing tomatoes for freezing by taking off the skins after dipping tomatoes briefly in boiling water. This works well in theory, less well in practice, for the process brings with it scalded fingers and much mess. We persevered with this method for a few years, stacking styrofoam trays full of nude tomatoes in the freezer and bringing them out in winter for soups and stews.

Then I had a stroke of genius (I like genius as a way of describing a change which avoids mess and work). Now we simply wash the tomatoes clean, dry them, put them in the freezer on trays covered with plastic wrap, and, when we need them, bring them out to use. Soup stock is strained anyway, and this gets rid of the skins and seeds. We put up with these in stews, which are usually cooked for so long that the skins virtually disintegrate.

When we run out of trays, we empty some we have already used and put the frozen tomatoes into plastic bags. They don't stick together if the skins are on; sticking together was one of the problems with frozen tomatoes which had had the skins removed.

And then there is the music of frozen tomatoes. If a bag of frozen tomatoes is spilled by accident on the kitchen floor, each of them falls with a different resonant sound depending on its size.

I have almost always grown tall tomatoes – Grosse Lisse, Apollo, South Australian Mighty Red are my preferred varieties. Most years I have tried a grafted tomato as well, with varied success. The claim that the grafted tomato is freer of disease is not borne out by my experience, but the crop I have had from some of them has been remarkable. In the best year, a grafted tomato filled a trellis about 1.8 metres high and spread sideways to span about 2 metres, all carefully tied to the trellis. The fruit was not large – the size of the largest hen's egg – but I stopped counting when I had picked 200 tomatoes from this one plant.

Some of my Italian friends swear by Roma, a pear-shaped tomato with a tough, dark red skin, excellent for making tomato paste. It is not the best for salads, because of the toughness of the skin.

My neighbour John Rosemead once gave me seeds of his favourite Beefsteak tomato, and I was able to get this to grow. Huge fruit, full of palatable flesh with few seeds, but not a heavy cropper. The plants I grew had only three or four fruits, but huge. Even so, they were much smaller than a large tomato reported from England, in the *Guinness Book of Records*: 4 pounds 5 ounces (1.956 kilograms) grown by R. A. Butcher at Stockbridge, Hants. in 1981. That's a meal or two.

If I had to plant a bush tomato, I think Rouge de Marmande would be the one I'd choose. The flavour is good, and the bushes bear well, but as with all bush tomatoes a proportion of the fruit is lost by its contact with the ground, and the tomato has a crinkled, indented skin, often quite heavily folded. Some nursery catalogues insist that Rouge de Marmande should be staked.

We read about the cottonwool flavour of some bought fruit and vegetables, grown to ripen on their way to the point of sale, grown in uniform size for efficiency of packing. Home-grown tomatoes are not like this. The tomato variety that is most criticised is Floradade, a Florida-developed variety (Miami is in Dade County), beloved of packers and supermarket owners. It is grown in this country too. Recently this variety has begun to appear in the seedling trays in nurseries. I suppose it is catering to those who insist on having a tomato as regular and reliable as supermarket tomatoes, and who have lost the use of their taste buds!

I rarely saw a fresh tomato when I was a child in the North, but I was quite familiar with the ubiquitous tomato sauce. Perhaps I grew up like the character in Angela Thirkell's *Trooper to the Southern Cross* who confessed that it wasn't until he grew up, left the station and went to Sydney that he found out you shouldn't put tomato sauce in the soup. What he did find out, after a few posh meals in Sydney, he says, is that it is

Worcestershire sauce you put in the soup. Angela Thirkell wasn't all that keen on Australian cuisine, or on Australians.

There was very little good said about Australian food before the 1950s. In his witty book *So, You Want to Be an Australian*, Cyril Pearl described the regional dishes of the five mainland states. In each case it was Steak and Eggs and Tomato Sauce, cooked too long and served sloppily. Australians, like the people of the pampas, ate a lot of good steak back then, at that stage of our Argentinian journey.

Now, since the nation has become Mediterranean, it is tomato with everything. Just a glance at the shelves near the pasta in the supermarket will tell of the change that has happened. Lots of lovely sauces with names like 'Do-ray-mio' that are sung about on television. Where would our cuisine be without the tomato, which came to Europe from South America, probably via Mexico, in the 16th century? The family it comes from, the Solanaceae, provides many foods and drugs, including the potato, the eggplant, the capsicum and all the really hot peppers, tobacco, nightshade, petunias and the daturas.

A Rash Thing with Radishes

Radishes come in red and pink and white and purple and black. Some are almost sweet and some are spicy. There are radishes that drive deep roots 30 centimetres down, and there are plump round little radishes that almost sit on the surface of the soil. What they all have in common is that their seed germinates quickly and the vegetable grows so rapidly that a family cannot keep up with it. The roots grow dry and spongy long before all the patch can be eaten.

A radish was the object of my most embarrassing vegetable experiment ever.

For some years I had read about the black Spanish radish, but its seeds were never on the racks in the nurseries I went to. Then I decided to get the catalogues of some seed companies that sell mainly through mail order, and there it was. Black Spanish radish.

It grew well. The roots tasted beautiful and tangy, but the flesh itself was near white. Only the skin was a thin film of black. Sliced, and in a salad, they looked inviting and very different.

From somewhere the idea came into my head that I should preserve some of them for later feasting. I imagine I looked at the radishes increasing in size by the day, and wanted to ensure that I had them longer than a couple of weeks.

So I pickled some in vinegar. I topped and tailed some black radishes, sliced them very thinly, and put them in a jar with vinegar and mustard seed. When I sampled them a few days later I knew I had a winner.

The point of this story springs from the fact that my olfactory sense has been somewhat faulty, for years. I just don't smell what other people smell.

One morning I packed a light lunch for work – some bread and meat, and a small lidded container of my pickled radishes. I went to the staffroom early for lunch as I had a commitment with some students later in lunchtime. I ate my meal with nobody else around.

When others arrived for lunch, they complained of a foul smell in the staffroom. Some said they could smell it at the other end of the corridor. I couldn't smell it, but it was my radishes. I beat an embarrassed retreat, trailing a disgusting whiff of hydrogen sulphide gas behind me.

The acid of the vinegar had reacted with the chemicals which formed the black skin of the Spanish radish. What I didn't know then, and do now, is that the black skin ought to be peeled off.

I still sow black radish seeds sometimes, but I never preserve them. Peeled, and then sliced into thin strips with a potato peeler, they are a tasty addition to a coleslaw. (Overweight and inedible red radishes are still useful, too; I slice the skin off with a potato peeler or zester and use this to add colour to coleslaw.)

From time to time I grow for my father-in-law Munich beer radishes and the white Japanese Daikon radish. These both have huge roots. He eats largely vegetarian meals, and likes to chop up one of these radishes and boil it lightly with a few other vegetables (or pieces of fruit) into a healthy mix.

Radishes (*Raphanus sativus*) have an honourable antiquity. They originated in western China and India, being cultivated in China in the 7th century BC. Radishes, onions and garlic formed the staple diet of the slaves who were building the pyramids, and the Greeks used to offer bowls of radishes to Apollo. According to Pliny, they had radishes made of gold in the temple of Apollo at Delphi.

The practical Romans used to throw radishes at politicians. There's a long comic history of expressing a political point of view through fruit and vegetable projectiles. It makes sense to use a vegetable as cheap and abundant as the radish for electoral purposes.

Radishes are so quick and easy to grow that anyone with a small piece of garden can grow some. They lose their crispness quickly in the carriage from field to market stall.

The radish is one of the vegetables customarily tortured for table decorations. It is easily carved and so cheap that mistakes are affordable.

Very Sexy Veg

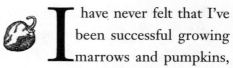 I have never felt that I've been successful growing marrows and pumpkins, but the reason is simply that I have never used any of the open areas of the garden, preferring to keep this for sweet corn, carrots, lettuce, and the like. I've used the odd spaces and corners instead. There was the gutter behind the shed – about a metre wide, a drain in winter, always damp in summer, but getting only a couple of hours' sun per day. There was an area next to the bird cages, between the cages and the first shrub, where the vines could climb the cages (they didn't) or ramble under the shrubs along the western side of the yard (they did, but there was not enough sun for them). The best place I've been prepared to use has been a strip about 10 metres long and a metre wide on the eastern side of the yard. This patch has given me between six and ten pumpkins – I usually plant Queensland blue – each year.

However, this is probably one of the least fertile patches in the garden, its goodness robbed by the neighbours' trees just across the fence. It did get good afternoon sun. Each year I used this area I began by barrowing in a large quantity of compost in various stages of decay, forming a more or less continuous hill which I covered with soil from elsewhere in the garden, until the hill was about 25 centimetres above the level of the path.

Meanwhile, I started the seeds off in containers. For pumpkins I used milk cartons, orange juice cartons, and two-litre wine cask cartons. I sliced the tops off, filled them two-thirds full with mixed compost and soil, planted the seeds and left them where I would see them and be reminded to water them. I punched holes in the bottom for drainage and for the roots to break through. All this was invented on the principle that these cartons were going to rot down themselves as the plants grew.

When they were big enough, I thinned out the seedlings if that was necessary, and planted them, still in the cartons, on the hill I had prepared, and forgot them as they grew, except for watering. I don't let weeds among pumpkins worry me, as they soon get smothered by the growing vines.

There are always huge numbers of male flowers, and in most seasons there are plenty of bees anxious to get about the task of pollinating. Female flowers are much less common, and tend to grow in more hidden places under the canopy of the leaves. They are fertile only for a day or so, and if the bees have not reached them with pollen from a male flower, they will shrivel without growing. So I developed the habit of pollinating them artificially so that they didn't miss out.

This can be done with a paint brush, using it to lick a

few grains of pollen from a male flower and transfer them to the female. The alternative method is to pluck off a male flower, strip back the petals, and apply the pollen directly by thrusting the stamen into the female flower. This is mildly titillating, for the male part fits so neatly into the female part that it is almost analogous to the human arrangement and it is not possible to get that idea out of the mind while the operation is being done. It little matters that what evolution has done is to fit out the female flower to entice not the male stamen, but the crawling bee, to enter it.

Some people eat marrow flowers, and there are recipes in several books. I've seen the dish once on an Adelaide restaurant menu, and some of my Italian friends who have eaten them speak well of the dish. Quite often it is zucchini flowers which are used, and the recipe is simple.

The flowers are washed, dried, and cut to spread flat, before being dipped into a smooth batter of flour, water and salt, and then quickly deep-fried in very hot vegetable oil. If you prefer, the salt can be sprinkled on after cooking rather than put in the batter.

I gave up growing zucchini after a few seasons. I tried the black ones, I tried the golden ones, I tried the grey-striped ones, in each case with overwhelming success. Overwhelming, because there is a limit to any family's patience when confronted with ratatouille and variations of ratatouille on a daily basis just to keep the gardener happy. I grew too many, they grew too big because we couldn't keep ahead of them, and the only other possibility besides the dreaded ratatouille was a pallid little cold salad of lightly boiled zucchini dressed in vinegar and oil. Freezing it for winter soups was not realistic, as it is far too watery a vegetable.

Zucchini are post-Second World War immigrants. *Zucca* is a pumpkin in Italian; *zucchini* is a diminutive form and is the plural of *zucchino*. Since nobody would ever buy just one of these tiny marrows, the possibility of committing a grammatical error in an Italian fruit shop probably doesn't exist. If you did, you might be considered *una zucca vuota*: a blockhead, literally an empty marrow.

One year I tried to grow button squash, but I didn't persist, though we liked the vegetable. I remember that it had plenty of flowers but few of them produced fruit.

The New Guinea bean came my way when I found a seedling in a pot at a garden shop, and I planted it on a trellis, 2 metres by 2 metres approximately, and it covered the whole area. Just once, and never again. The main product was a mass of small fruit the size and shape of a bean, which could be steamed and eaten; those which were not eaten almost all shrivelled and fell off before they reached pencil length. The two or three survivors fattened to about 5 centimetres in diameter and grew to a metre in length, and were as uninteresting to eat as the zucchini. The vine produced a mountain of useful compost in the end.

I think there were more varieties of pumpkin and marrow (I've always used the words interchangeably, which is wrong) when I was a child, but today the overwhelming popularity of Queensland blue and butternut has almost driven the others out of sight. I remember the triamble, with its three lobes, so hard to peel efficiently, and the extraordinarily coloured Turk's head, with its turban.

In North America, the pumpkin has been assimilated into folk practices at Hallowe'en, hollowed out and carved and with a candle inside, representing some archetypal horror figure. Though Australian children are thoroughly familiar with the images of the Hallowe'en pumpkin from television and comic books, the actual artifact has not been developed here, because the seasons are turned on their head in our hemisphere. In North America, November is the start of winter, and the pumpkins, which have grown through summer and ripened through autumn, are in store and readily available – at least they were in the century the practice grew up. I doubt they are much stored in the suburbs of contemporary America. So we don't have it here, not the pumpkins anyway, but we do have the confectionery manufacturers and a few others trying to give us yet another commercial festival, and each year the streets of my suburb see a few more children doorknocking for trick or treat.

I have a friend who lives in a small town on the River Murray, and for a second income grows pumpkins on the farmlet he owns. It is a welcome income supplement from a crop that doesn't take much looking after and isn't attacked by birds the way grapes and apricots are. When the pumpkins are ripe, the vines die and the vegetables can be picked up easily and at leisure. One year, however, just before he was ready to collect the crop, there came a freak late summer rainstorm, a flash flood, and away went his pumpkins, into the river, in their thousands, floating and bobbing colourfully among all the other debris washed down by the storm. On television it looked ludicrous; it wasn't so for him.

Cleaning up in my back yard garden after the pumpkins are ready to store is fairly easy. I chop the vines into pieces, throw them in a pile, and spade soil on top of them. They rot quickly. As I clean up I keep an eye on the wildlife that has been living under the vines, and in that way I dispatch a good number of the snails that have been hiding in the dense shade and dampness getting ready to breed and march forth in cooler weather.

I reached the conclusion recently that I cannot afford to grow pumpkins any more. They take a great deal of water, and recently the water rating system in South

Australia has changed so drastically that there is now some pain in using water on a vegetable garden. Something has to go.

My family's favourite way of eating marrow is probably boiled and mashed with potatoes: yellow potatoes we called it when they were young. The runner-up is a dish we have recently developed: marrow dipped into cream mixed with salt and Malaysian curry, and then baked in the oven. This method is good for wedges of potato, onion, carrot and cauliflower, as well as for marrow, and the leftovers are just as good cold.

Pollination

The trouble with marrows is simply sex:
male flowers, female flowers, and bees.
The bees to someone else's garden have gone
and lie about sipping from grapes. Here

the female flowers are anxious to get heavy
with winter veg. And it's simple, really.
One small brush, relic from a painting course
I didn't finish, pushed into a male flower

and the stamen stroked for a brushload
of pollen. It is necessary to know
when to stop. Transfer pollen and brush
to the waiting pistil, and tickle,

but gently does it. Marrows may prove
too rampant for most gardens, says
Mr Yates. Agreed. Should they pollinate
bucking and writhing in tangles alive

with tendrils, there'd be an injunction
slapped on my quarter-acre. As it is,
I don't do the delicate work with a brush
if the neighbour's around. He'd want to lean

over the fence and look. Even on ABC
the garden adviser carries a leer
when he describes the task. I think
they'd beep him out if he undertook

to tell the other way: direct contact
of torn-off stamen and female flower,
and you, the novice gardener, must take care
that the hand doesn't shake. The lady

welcomes these attentions for a day,
or shrivels unfertilised. Now let me tell:
in Southern Europe old men pick these flowers
and eat them, cooked in batter, for a feast.

Coping with Chillies

In my social studies class one year my students were overwhelmingly Italian–Australians, and our discussions in the unit on 'Work' were wide-ranging. One day we were talking about men's and women's work in the home, and talk turned to gardening. Many of the boys had had to help their fathers in their gardens (the whole suburb had been built on old market gardens and in a walk around the perimeter of the school grounds we could see feral beetroot and silver beet still surviving and adapted to the frequent passage of the gang mower). The garden was not unknown to the girls, for in many cases it was the mothers who looked after the garden and their daughters were required to assist with the tomato processing and other annual activities.

We swapped gardening experiences, mine and theirs, for a while; a day later Mario brought me a packet of the hot peppers his father grew, so that I could try them.

We were not used to hot peppers with our food, and tried them very tentatively with a casserole – just a single chilli cooked with it, and then taken out. Since then, little by little, we have become used to them, and we are now able to accept the bite of chilli in food.

I still grow chillies – hot peppers – descended from

Mario's dad's peppers, because I dried and kept some of the seed, and raised a few plants every year.

Without Columbus and the Conquistadors, without the several varieties of the *Capsicum* family, the cuisine of many parts of the world would be much different, for the chilli provides the spicy heat in many cuisines on all continents.

Archaeologists know that wild chillies were being used in central Mexico as much as 7,000 years ago, and the plant had been domesticated in Peru by 2,500 BC. Among the Aztecs in Mexico, chillies were used in the cookery of all classes. They were used fresh, and also dried, smoked, or turned into powder or paste.

The Aztecs didn't have plastic gloves, or goggles for their eyes, both of which are required equipment for people involved in the commercial preparation of the strongest, hottest chillies. If the juice of a chilli gets on the hands, it can cause a burning sensation for a day or more, and can be passed on by touching someone else as well. I know from bitter experience the danger of touching the eyes or the nasal membranes after handling chillies.

The hot part of the chilli is in the pith at the centre of the fruit, and to a lesser extent in the seeds, both of which contain minute quantities of the chemical capsaicin. The skin contains the aromatic flavours which distinguish the capsicum and all its chilli cousins.

The ability to become resistant to the hotness, through familiarity with it, is a problem for the commercial grading of chillies. Testers cannot be habitual eaters of foods containing chilli. Testers grade subjectively (the chemical occurs in such tiny quantities as to defy analytical grading) and use Scoville Heat Units in the range from 0 to 60,000 units. The range from 20,000 upwards is reserved for the hottest. Since tabasco starts at 20,000 units, I can't imagine what some of the hottest wild varieties and hybrid cultivars must be like to merit 60,000 Scoville Heat Units.

We use chillies (in moderation unless my hand or my judgment slips) in casseroles, and in the minced meat for rissoles. The bright red enlivens rissoles as much as the green of parsley does. When I make soup stock from chicken carcasses, I always throw two or three chillies into the boiling.

There are several ways I preserve chillies for use during the year.

1. Sometimes I pull up the whole plant and hang it upside down in a dry place, under wide eaves or in the shed. The last green ones ripen as the plant slowly dies, and the fruits can be pulled off as they are needed.

2. Old shoe boxes abound in our shed, and never get thrown in the bin. I line a box with tissues or some sort of kitchen paper, and put a layer of chillies in the bottom. They dry slowly in a semi-dark place.

3.   Sometimes I pick the fruit – or just break off sections of the ripening plant – and pack them into plastic bags, seal them, and drop them into the freezer. They are just as potent twelve months later.

4.   Chillies keep well if they are packed in vinegar. I slit them open so that the vinegar can get inside them, otherwise they want to float.

5.   I also slit them open when I pack them in oil. This is my favourite method now, because they keep indefinitely, and after twelve months or so the oil takes on an orange-coloured glow and has such hotness itself that, used in quite tiny quantities, it is an admirable addition to any frying or roasting, or to salads.

Once I brushed a beef roast with the oil I had kept chillies in, and then dusted it with a fragrant, but not hot, curry powder before roasting it. The beef was most beautifully flavoured, but I had been far too heavy-handed and the gravy which Tina made was so strong it would have stripped paint. I had gone far beyond the family's tolerance, or mine, for that matter.

When I have an excess of chillies, which is most years,

I pack the spare into plastic sandwich bags and leave them on a table at work for anyone who wants them. They always go quickly.

My friend Frank, who with his family runs the best Italian grocery in the city, grows chillies at home, and each year strings them in braids and pretty clusters and hangs them from the rafters in his shop. Their bright red colour makes them as much art as grocery, and they slowly dry there, above the hanging provolone and salami and the shining display of European stainless steel cooking utensils, which every decent Italian grocer's shop displays.

The word *chilli* comes from a Nahuatl word of southern Mexico and Central America. That's a continent away from the country called Chile, and obviously therefore not the origin of that country's name. A map produced by a Chilean government agency says that before the arrival of Europeans, the Aconcagua Valley of central Chile was the only area bearing the name; as the conquistadors extended their control they named the whole area Chile. At least three theories exist for its original meaning – perhaps the name of a native chieftain in the Aconcagua Valley, perhaps the name of a river in the vicinity, perhaps the trill of an indigenous bird. I like the last.

So *chile* is an alternative spelling for the fruit, along with *chili*. The word *chili* in North Africa is the name of a hot, dry sirocco wind; this is a Berber word and has nothing at all, except coincidence, to do with the small hot capsicum. However, North African cuisine makes extensive use of spice mixtures of which hot chilli is one of the main ingredients.

I have said nothing about ordinary capsicums, which we grow in abundance each year, and eat with the muted enthusiasm families always apply to vegetables that are good for you.

Companion Planting

The English Romantic poet John Keats wrote a poem which is probably the best-known literary use of a garden herb. This is 'Isabella; or The Pot of Basil', which uses a 14th century story from Boccaccio and retells it in verse, in sixty-three eight-line stanzas full of love and murder and a ghost and some macabre goings-on. And a plant of basil that is a key player in a mystery.

Isabella was the sister of two rich Florentines who are briefly described as owners of mines and factories and ships, and employers of workers little better than slaves. Capitalist villains, in fact. They also see themselves as owners of their sister Isabella, whom they plan to use to make a strategic marriage to 'some high noble and his olive-trees'.

This kind of engineered alliance of the merchant class with the aristocracy has obviously a long lineage. In the 20th century the olive trees would then be bulldozed to make way for a housing estate with an up-market name.

When the brothers discovered that Isabella had fallen in love with Lorenzo, a man who worked for them in their trading business, they took him out hunting, killed him and buried him in the forest. Isabella pined for his absence, and the brothers, being tough operators, weren't about to give their game away. So Keats had to get the story moving towards its resolution by the device of sending Lorenzo's ghost to visit Isabella and tell her what had happened to him.

Isabella, who must have had some of her brothers' tough-mindedness, went into the forest with her nurse, dug up the corpse, and cut off the head. She took it home and spent some time combing the hair, pointing the eyelashes, and washing off the dirt with her tears. Then she hid the head in a pot, covering it with potting soil and sowing a basil plant on top of it.

A domestically minded woman looking after a pot of basil would not have been considered remarkable anywhere in Italy. To this day, Italians keep basil in pots indoors and make sure it is placed where it can collect sunlight through a window.

What drew attention to Isabella's basil was the fact that she watered it with her tears, all day long, rarely left it except for brief necessary purposes skimmed over delicately by Keats, and, because she was neither eating nor sleeping, grew increasingly anorexic in appearance.

> And so she ever fed it with thin tears,
> Whence thick, and green, and beautiful it grew,
> So that it smelt more balmy than its peers
> Of Basil-tufts in Florence; for it drew
> Nurture besides, and life, from human fears,

From the fast mouldering head there shut from view:
So that the jewel, safely casketed,
Came forth, and in perfumed leafits spread.

The suspicious brothers took the pot away, dug it up, and discovered the head, now 'vile with green and livid spot'. At this point Boccaccio and Keats intrude what seems to me a false note. The brothers fled from Florence and never came back.

Given what Keats says earlier about their mercantile ruthlessness, it would have been more in character for them to tough it out. After all, they had possession of the material evidence. One of the witnesses was Isabella's aged nurse, who disappeared from the story, probably having expired from the effects of spending three hours digging up a corpse in a damp forest. The other witness was Isabella herself, now noticeably loony. They could have afforded to buy all the influence they needed to impede investigation if anyone heard their sick sister and paid attention to her.

She spent the last two stanzas pining away until she died forlorn!

Historically, young Italian women wore sprigs of sweet basil in their bosoms, believing that this would engender sympathy. Perhaps Isabella should have done this instead of planting her young man's head on the window sill.

Putting your lover's head in a pot of basil may be

considered a form of companion planting, I suppose.

I do know from my experience growing basil that the pot she used was far too large for a single plant, unless Lorenzo had a very tiny head. I suspect that the salty water of her tears probably would not have done much good for the plant.

I grow basil every year. It is essential with a salad of tomatoes and onions or cucumber, and it is essential with any dish of cooked tomatoes, or sauces made from tomatoes. With pasta dishes we often use pesto, that tangy sauce made of basil, garlic, olive oil, and a combination of sheep's milk cheese with Parmesan cheese.

I tried to make pesto, both with a mortar and pestle and in a blender, but was not happy with the results, and so we get our pesto from Norwood's Italian grocer, who makes his own.

Unfortunately basil runs to seed early in the season, and so I usually make three successive sowings. Keeping basil for use during the winter is a challenge. Because neither the colour nor flavour of dried basil is good enough, I use the freezer. Some I put away just as it is plucked, in leafy branches, stuffed into plastic bags. I usually use a double plastic bag, as the first is likely to be pierced by the stalks. Some I strip of leaves and freeze these with water in ice cube trays, and then pile them into plastic bags in the freezer. Either of these is good for winter cooking with tomatoes.

I have tried bush basil, dark opal basil, and some of the scented basils (clove, aniseed) but I keep coming back to the reliable and prolific sweet basil and lettuce-leaf basil. I get some of my plants from those which spring up naturally in the garden. At the end of one season, the old plants will be used for mulch and there are always seeds in the soil. In addition, I scatter seeds such as basil throughout the garden if I have any left.

As soon as the basil bush flowers, there are always bees in profusion. Plucking basil for the kitchen needs some care.

Basil (the herb), basilica (the church), basilisk (the reptile) and Basil (the boy's name) are all related. The words come from ancient Greek *basilikos*, meaning 'kingly'.

So basil, known to science as *Ocimum basilicum*, is the kingly plant, and has been in Europe since ancient times. The French even call it *herbe royale*. Its native home is in India, where it is a sacred herb.

In English, basil seems to have dignity if you think of the herb, but there has always been something comic about Basil as a given name. The comical connotations of Basil are now firmly fixed for a generation, thanks to John Cleese's hilarious portrayal of Basil Fawlty.

Yet in Eastern Europe, Basil and its variations such as Vasily have an honourable history. There have been emperors and theologians and saints bearing the name.

In Moscow is the Cathedral of St Basil the Blessed, that marvellously photogenic building with its multi-coloured onion-shaped domes. This ecclesiastical architecture looks to me like faulty towers.

Herb of Grace O' Sundays

'There's fennel for you, and columbines; there's rue for you; and here's some for me; we may call it herb of grace o' Sundays. O! you must wear your rue with a difference. There's a daisy; I would give you some violets, but they withered all when my father died. They say he made a good end.'

Poor Ophelia, going mad with an armful of herbs and flowers, scattering them as if for her father's funeral and on her way to her own death shortly afterwards.

I first met the herb rue in Shakespeare, when I studied *Hamlet*. Surrounding the sad figure of Ophelia throughout the play are conflicting images of carnality and spirituality, and so it is appropriate that she also gives the alternative English name of the plant, herb of grace.

Centuries ago, a sprig of rue was used in Catholic churches to scatter holy water on the congregation, hence, presumably, its name herb of grace. This in turn sprang from ancient beliefs about the ability of rue to ward off evil.

Rue is too bitter to be used in cooking, but historically has been used in medicines. However, it is poisonous in large amounts, and must not be taken during pregnancy, because it has an abortive action. Whatever its value medically, its astringency is enough to convince the converted that it must be of value. Some people swear by it for keeping insects away.

Having met rue in literature, I forgot about it. The first time I saw it in real life, it was drowned. Yes, in a bottle of grappa, a substantial piece of it floating in the bottom half of the bottle. This is a customary European use for rue, to give a desired flavour to this particular firewater. My host Fausto explained what it was to me, but he used the Italian name *ruta*, which is identical to the Latin name, and it was some time before I realised that ruta and rue were the same plant.

Ruta, or rue, soggy in a bottle of grappa, has a misleading dark appearance, but the plant I saw in a pot at a fete was different. The pinnate leaves are a light smoky green in a delicate pattern. I paid my two dollars, took the plant home, and transplanted it into a border I used for herbs.

Rue grows very slowly at first, I discovered, but eventually reaches up to a metre, and is a quite showy bush. It is a perennial which has a delicate four-part flower, succeeded in turn by a four-lobed seed-case. The bush grew for several years, and every time I brushed past it or weeded near it I got a whiff of its distinct pungency. Finally it died and joined the rest of my compost.

About three years later another rue plant appeared, a seedling near where its parent had grown. This suggests to me that the seeds can stay in the soil ready to germinate for quite some time. I transplanted it to a place near the tap, and ignored it. When I sowed some hills of Queensland blue marrows on that side of the yard, it almost disappeared under the rampant vines, but survived and sent up flower heads above the sea of marrow leaves.

Rue can be used in dried flower arrangements: the pale yellow flowers stay yellow, the leaves hold on and retain most of their greyish-green, and the distinct quadruple bulbs of the seed-cases, small as they are, are unusual shapes. From the point of view of drying it for flowers, the plant which had survived among the marrows was valuable, for the weight and strength of the marrow vines forced distortions on the normal erectness of the rue, and these twisted shapes made interesting arrangements.

Rue is known to science as *Ruta graveolens – graveolens* meaning 'strong-smelling' – and is one of a family of shrubs and herbs called the Rutaceae. They are natives of Europe, adjacent parts of Asia, and the Canary Islands. *Ruta graveolens* is one of several well-acclimatised plants and animals originally taken to Britain by the Romans, who I presume took it along for much the same reason expatriate Australians like to have Vegemite to hand.

The books on companion planting say that rue and basil are incompatible, and it is the tender basil which succumbs.

It would be nice to think that the verb 'to rue' is related to the name of the bitter herb, but not so. The verb comes from the Old English *hreowan*, 'to be sorry'; the name of the herb comes from its name in Latin, *ruta*. It is found in Cicero and Ovid, and is used by Cicero as an image of bitterness and unpleasantness.

However, the apparent kinship of the two rues has led to some delightful punning. An 18th century book of proverbs quotes two proverbs that depend on the pun, and also on a pun on the other herb thyme. Thus 'Rue and thyme grow both in one garden' seems to me rather obscure, but somewhere in it is the idea of repenting before time runs out. 'Rue in thyme should be a maiden's posie' would be understood by poor Ophelia, who was not alone in literature or in life in finding that love turned sour.

Then there was Sir Walter Scott, who must have tasted rue or an infusion of it, to lead him to use the image in a poem.

A weary lot is thine, fair maid,
A weary lot is thine!
To pull the thorn thy brow to braid
And press the rue for wine.

Wine made from rue would be several steps below parsnip wine in palatability.

Tarragon Vinegar

This poem starts with a recipe for you:
tarragon vinegar is easy to make. You need
white vinegar, a flagon, and you cut
handfuls of tarragon out of the herb
in the side garden. Simply stuff it
down in the flagon, replace the lid,
and leave it out there in the sun.

The sun is the trick: the heat will draw
out the essence of tarragon, and soon,
diffused through the vinegar, that taste
will serve you salads all the year.

Three weeks in the sun will do.

There's a little more has to be done than that. After the
flagons have stood in the sun (hot January and February
are best) the liquor has to be filtered and then bottled.
I use small soft drink and soda water bottles. Then I
add a fresh sprig of tarragon to the new bottle, and put it
away till we use it.

When I was still involved with school fetes, I made
dozens of bottles of herb vinegar. They sold quickly.
Commercial prices are usually exorbitant.

We use herb vinegar with every salad. Other varieties

we have made are with rosemary, thyme, garlic chives, and orange peel. Tarragon vinegar is without a doubt the whole family's favourite.

I use a similar process to make a tangy garlic and pepper oil. Simply add hot peppers and chopped garlic to a container of oil, and leave it in a dark place (not in the sun) for a couple of months, stirring the oil by turning the bottle occasionally. After that the garlic should come out lest it turn rancid.

Early in my life as a gardener, I was caught by the trap many novice gardeners fall into. I bought a plant of tarragon, which grew prolifically, but I couldn't work out why all the gardening writers raved about it until someone told me I had Russian tarragon. I hunted around until I found French tarragon, with its delicate aniseed smell, and I haven't looked back since.

Russian tarragon is to French tarragon as Russian cooking is to French cuisine.

Tarragon is known to the French as *estragon*, to the Spaniards as *tarragón* or *estragón*, to the Italians as *targone* or *dragoncello*, and to botanists as *Artemisia dracunculus*. *Dracunculus* is the diminutive of the Latin word for dragon. Though these words all look related, and are, the Spanish form probably came from an Arabic word, and that in turn from the Greek word for dragon.

Since *dragon* is at the heart of the etymology of all these words, I am amused that Samuel Beckett used

Estragon as the name of a character in his play *Waiting for Godot*. Estragon is a mild, passive victim of life, almost frozen into inaction. Was Beckett being ironical?

Rosemary Remembered

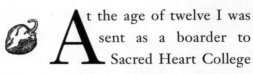At the age of twelve I was sent as a boarder to Sacred Heart College at Somerton Park, where the boarding school run by the Marist Brothers was in a former stately home called Paringa Hall. The remains of the old garden were slowly deteriorating under the impact of boys in large numbers; one relic was the dull gray, low hedge along the curving drives.

This was rosemary, and this was how Australians used to use the plant, as a garden plant, for its attractive foliage, or as a hedge for its hardiness. In England, rosemary was considered a useful plant for low mazes and for knot gardens, for the same reasons. The rosemary hedge at Sacred Heart College, however, was making heavy weather of it, and there were gaps and untidy patches, caused by a local custom.

The local custom consisted of picking up a boy – new and preferably small – and dropping him into the hedge. Crushed rosemary has a strong smell, which lasts all day on a grey melange suit, rendering the victim a pariah. If the monks caught us at it, there was trouble, but keeping out of sight of the monks was an agreed objective. In their sight, we all behaved, and called them Brothers.

My mother's generation of Australian cooks hardly

knew about herbs, with the exception of thyme, which was used with chicken. We didn't call it chicken then; we called it roast fowl, it was always stuffed with a bread and thyme mixture, and it was provided as a special treat on important occasions. In our house, it was often a bird we knew by name or laying habits, unless it was a superfluous rooster getting his comeuppance.

Not many Australians used rosemary in cooking before the post-war influx of Southern European immigrants. Now it is extremely common, and much loved. We always push rosemary and pieces of garlic into little pockets we cut into lamb roasts.

I maintain three rosemary bushes at various stages in the yard. One of them has to be near the house – Tina expects the herb bed to be easily reached from the kitchen. One of them survives at the end of the yard, north-east of the shed by the downpipe, and is never watered. Another I will use for propagation, which I do in the simplest way possible. I bend some low branches of the rosemary to the ground, and put a spade or two of soil over these to pin them down. If I keep this damp, in a few months a good root system develops on the branch and I can cut off the new rosemary bush to plant it out somewhere else.

'There's rosemary, that's for remembrance; pray, love, remember' said Ophelia in her mad scene in *Hamlet*. She gave the herb to her brother Laertes, asking him to remember what had happened to her and echoing the Ghost's injunction to Hamlet. It was the ancient Greeks, among others, who saw rosemary as an aid to remembering and clear-headedness, and the oil of rosemary has been an ingredient in a number of curative and refreshing recipes, including eau-de-cologne.

We just use it with lamb, and in rosemary vinegar.

Rosemary

The sight of rosemary yanks me back to time
when the trick was to dump the new boy
into the trimmed border along the drive
at Paringa Hall. Its scrupulous curves
could not conceal the gaps where boys
were thrown. The victim was sentenced to stink
all day. That took place so long ago
and in another country I remember, called
salt-and-pepper-and-mustard Australia,
long before the invasion of herbs.

Tamarillo

The first year we had a good crop of tamarillos from our tree, I used to take half a dozen to work with me to eat for lunch (slice open, scoop out with a spoon) and my colleagues would drool. I found out why the first time I saw them on sale in a fruit shop – at 95 cents each, for an egg-shaped, egg-sized bright red fruit.

The tamarillo has a tough skin, and a red flesh not unlike a passionfruit, that is, pulp and seeds. The fruit hangs in small groups from the tree, developing from tiny, highly scented flowers. The taste is pleasantly tart, and the fruit keeps well.

This plant (*Cyphomandra betacea*) is another of the South American connections in our garden, a short-lived small tree with large leaves, quite prone to wind damage but not, in my experience, particularly avid for water. It is often sold as a tree tomato. It has been cultivated in Ecuador and Peru since ancient times, and is found also in Brazil.

We got this plant from Josephine, an Italian woman who used to clean for us. Josephine was an avid gardener, and very knowledgeable. She and I swapped ideas, seeds, seedlings, and produce; and one day she brought me an undistinguished piece of tree, told me what it was, and suggested I plant it. I put it in a bare and unprofitable bed in front of the lounge room window, hoping it would fill the space and provide shade.

It put down roots and grew, but did not thrive in the stony soil. So I moved it to the back of the yard, and in no time it was a tree about 2 metres high, covered in red fruit.

In the season I decided I would cash in on the fruit, we were in a fruit fly quarantine area and that plan had to be dropped. Then the tree began to sicken and was at the end of its life. I tried to raise another from seed, without luck, and despite the quantities of unused fruit which had joined the compost, no young tamarillos sprang up.

So I bought another from a nursery specialising in exotic fruit, put it in, surrounded it with a mound of compost to enrich the soil, and watched it grow while I waited, with my teaspoon ready, for the first new fruit to ripen. It grew splendidly, set a lot of fruit, and then, overnight, lost half its boughs under the weight of the unripe fruit. The survivors look as if they will be ready soon, and the tree has already put on new growth to replace what it lost.

This time I have started a new tree from a cutting before the tamarillo expires. Unless it has been grafted onto a wild tobacco rootstock, the tamarillo dies within four to six years, and may indeed die at two or three years if nematode infestation of the roots gets too bad.

Plum Sunday

These are the January nights
when the ripe plums fall
under the tree, six one night,
nine the next, such glut.

Such temporary gluttons
in the house. I fill the bowl
and all evaporate, save stones
which travel to odd spots,

(arm of chair, top of book),
save stains on T-shirts.
Think rich red sweet flesh
and you think of plum;

lick the side of mouth
lest it drain down to beard.
These are the rare plums sung
in Persian rhyme, gilded

by legends out of the east
until all expectation
hangs on the waiting day.
If the month turns cold,

the year waits, the mouth
waits for the prized juice;
the essence that plumps
the fruit full is on hold.

When the heat returns
to the season, the last
secret lacquer and shine
are applied to the skin.

Some mornings are chill,
that early stillness I like;
I pick up the fallen fruit
and it seems ice-cold.

I rub dust on my sleeve
and the plums glow, alive,
they're alive with longing
for the cut-glass bowl

where the light plays games
through the facets, and plums
are Chinese lanterns red
with energy, ruby-stone

viewed through a glass,
hibiscus, the boldest,
reflected in water:
all of that simple plum.

I will pass December
in a gallop, to wait in sun
for January's days of full,
round, ripe, succulent plum.

Night and Plums

Plums, in this late evening light,
hide, engross themselves,
lodged in a globular clutter of leaves
reeling in focus, lost
in a black dimension.
The silhouette of tree
under the pinned pearl of evening cloud
hides and conceals: purple and green
become black clusters
on branches, moved, moving,
in wind and rising cloud and moon.

Plums are good men plucked in light.
The soft plot of their fall,
by night, confounds.

The Carthaginian Dwarf

The Latin poet Pliny was mistaken about the origins of the pomegranate, and so he called it *malum punicum*, the Carthaginian apple.

Almost certainly it grew around Carthage, because it grew wild all around the Mediterranean, but it is native to western Asia. Since Carthage was a Phoenician settlement, the fruit would have come with them. However, after the Romans had finished with Carthage, nothing was intended to grow there, ever again, when the Romans burnt the city, ploughed the ruins under, and salted the soil.

Mohammed said, 'Eat the pomegranate, for it purges the system of envy and hatred'. There is no doubt that its juice has a freshness and slight astringency that is cleansing on the palate.

Solomon, who had more than his fair share of the good things of life, had an orchard of pomegranates. In the 'Song of Songs', part of the description of a beautiful girl is 'thy cheeks show through their veil rosy as a halved pomegranate'. In more lover's talk in the 'Song of Songs', spiced wine brewed freshly from pomegranates was full of sensual promise.

When Moses promised the Israelites wandering in

the desert a new land to live in, it was more than milk and honey he spoke of. His promise, in Deuteronomy, was 'a land of wheat and barley, of vine and fig-tree and pomegranate and olive'. It sounds like the best produce of the Mediterranean climate of South Australia.

Various meanings have been attached to the pomegranate as a symbol. In Christian tradition, the pomegranate has sometimes stood for the unified Church, sometimes for resurrection and fertility. For the ancient Greeks, it represented conjugal love and fruitfulness and rejuvenation. Their goddess Hera, wife of Zeus, carried a pomegranate in her left hand.

Apples, oranges, and grapes are often seen in paintings. I would nominate the pomegranate as the next most popular fruit with artists. Its shape, colour and sheen are a challenge to an artist; the shapes of white pith inset with seeds are visually interesting; and in some paintings the pomegranate is used symbolically. Moreover, the pomegranate is a durable fruit. Drop it on the floor, or leave it in the studio while you take a week's holiday, and it will still look the same.

There are pomegranates on the table and in the bowl in Renoir's 1881 painting *Fruits of the Midi* which is in the Art Institute of Chicago. In 1908 John Singer Sargent painted *Pomegranates*, now in the Brooklyn Museum; Sargent's fruit is on the tree, close to the viewer and hidden intricately in the depths of the foliage.

The German painter Lucas Cranach painted *The Fee* in 1532. It seems to be in a shop, for there is food on the counter and much game hanging from the walls. A woman is being paid coins by an old man with a lecherous leer about him. On the table is a pomegranate, broken open: faithfulness breached, I presume.

Jean-Baptiste-Siméon Chardin's *Grapes and Pomegranates* of 1763 has two pomegranates beside grapes and porcelain. One of the fruits has split open in a curious triple split; fully ripe pomegranates usually split on the tree.

The Christian symbolism of the pomegranate is probably intended in Botticelli's *Madonna of the Magnificat*, which is in the Uffizi Gallery in Florence. Mary and the Christ Child both have their left hands on a pomegranate, while Mary is writing some of the text of the Magnificat with her right hand. Of course, it may be that Botticelli was alluding to the myth of Hera.

The Australian painter Salvatore Zofrea was inspired by Cavafy's poem 'Waiting for the Barbarians' to paint a picture of the same name. The setting is a Mediterranean city with classical architecture; the far streets are deserted, and the remaining inhabitants, dressed magnificently and grotesquely, clustered in the square waiting for the inevitable annihilation when the barbarians come. Behind them is an immense pomegranate filling the square, split open along the side with the seeds ready to spill out. Zofrea's pomegranate, 3 metres high and just as wide, can be read in many ways. I see it as the death of the old – it is splitting open, fully ripe – and as the potential birth of the new.

That the pomegranate grows wild in places where it was first taken as a fruit tree is no surprise, because it is equipped with so many seeds, ideal for long-distance spitting competitions, that any picnic with pomegranates would have left behind enough to start a grove.

I've never had a pomegranate tree, but I always have the dwarf pomegranate, *Punica granatum nana*, which comes up like a weed all through the garden.

The dwarf pomegranate is a bright splash of colour in the garden, with bright green, small, glossy leaves, and the pink and red of the fruit like carnival lights. The over-ripe fruits fall, and are raked into the compost, and then young plants shoot up in many parts of the garden. They are very hardy, thrive when ignored, and bear most attractive red flower buds before the fruit develops. It is a worthwhile supplement to cut flowers.

For years we had three dwarf pomegranate bushes as the dominant plants in a small rockery (which we've now dismantled and replaced with a lime tree surrounded by bright orange and pink cannas).

Our parent plant has been growing beside the incinerator for well over twenty years. It is now over a metre high. Sometimes it has been scorched back when there has been a big fire in the incinerator, and has always revived.

Many years ago, when fruit fly control measures were first introduced to Adelaide, strippers used to visit properties in the proclaimed suburbs, and take everything that could act as host to the fruit fly. This included dwarf pomegranate fruits.

One year, when the strippers left, they gave us a form to fill out with our estimate of what was taken, for compensation. I filled out dwarf pomegranates under the heading Any Other Claims, gave a value, and waited for the inevitable rejection.

The two strippers who took away the dwarf pomegranate fruit were Poms, English immigrants. It is usually accepted that the slang term Australians use for English people derives from a cute piece of rhyming slang, *pomegranate/immigrant*. The fruit's name tells simply that it is a fruit (pome) with seeds.

Lilly Pilly

The lilly pilly tree is known to science as *Acmena smithii*, and was formerly *Eugenia smithii*. (I have seen another gardening book which claims it is *Eugenia smithii* and was formerly *Acmena smithii*!) It is a rainforest tree very common in northern Australia and also known through south-east China and the islands of Indonesia.

For a tree of rainforest origin, it does surprisingly well in the Adelaide suburbs, and its white or purple fruit can often be seen in local gardens.

Our block slopes slightly from east to west, as the eastern suburbs of Adelaide generally do, and I think it was quite likely that once there was a small watercourse running down the slope in wet weather, because at the end of the yard there is a wet-weather stream fairly well defined, but these days it collects its water from the eastern neighbour's paved yard. This flows through our yard, and into the next door neighbour's if the rain is very heavy. Usually the water gets no further than the corner where we had planted three lilly pilly trees, and I removed some of the topsoil from this corner to allow the stormwater to pond in this area. As a result, the lilly pilly trees, which we never watered, thrived right from the start.

These were beautiful trees. The glossy evergreen leaves are dense, and the growing tips are a rich bronze colour. In late spring, the trees are a mass of white blossoms, and then the flowers fall, a tiny rain of small white whisker-like parts which drift like a white powder over the ground, over the paving, over the washing. During the flowering season the trees are noisy with bees, and then the fruit sets. Ours had purple fruit, richly colourful, and cropped very heavily.

When the fruit was ripe in late summer, the trees were always visited by parrots. In late summer, there is little surface water even in the hills, and birds seek sweetness and liquid in gardens. The parrots hung in noisy groups in the lilly pilly trees and ate heartily and raucously. The berries are sweet, and quite juicy, and stay on the trees for a long time. But eventually they fall, and that's when the trouble starts.

The fruits fell in their thousands, shrivelled, rotted, and then, in spring, germinated. Because they were under the shade of the parent trees, they didn't survive to compete, but for a time they were like a green scum around the trees. More of a problem with the trees in our garden was the fall of the fruit onto the paving underneath the clothes line, the resulting squashed fruit and then the discomfort and danger of walking on the small stones within them. Birds' droppings, ripely coloured, were also a problem.

The fruit is edible; I liked it to chew when I was in the garden, but each berry is only a tiny mouthful, and half of that is the seed. It is sweet, with a slightly acid tang. It doesn't keep indoors, not that there's any need to. The pleasure is not in the flesh of the fruit, but in the juice from the flesh as it is chewed. Suck the juice and spit out the flesh and seed was what I did.

I'll try anything once, and so one summer I picked the best and plumpest fruit I could find, boiled it up with sugar, and strained and reduced the liquid. What I got was a sweet, dullish purple brew which I liked and no one else in the house would touch. I bottled it and used it on ice cream.

As our three trees grew, they forked out attractively and began putting on weight. Eventually two of the three were huge, with trunks about 40 centimetres in diameter. They were out of the way between the cubby and the fence, and as Grandpa pottered around among his collections of odds and ends he saw a way of conveniently storing old pipes and rails. Up they went, until there were a couple of hundredweights of old iron stored at head height between the trees, and old chains draped around the branches, no longer underfoot.

As they grew bigger and bigger, the problems also grew. There was too much shade over the clothes line. The spread of the branches soon meant that fruits were dropping onto the roof of the cubby-house and the gutters began to rust from the moistness of the rotting fruit, which fell in such quantities that my occasional efforts to keep these gutters clean were of no use. My neighbour gently described to me from time to time the effect of heavy shade and root intrusion on his little apple tree and on his attempts to grow vegetables.

So we decided that two of them had to go, nice as they were, leaving the smallest of the three, closest to the back fence. By now John and Andrew were in secondary school, and I asked Grandpa to let them do the work of taking out the first tree, which they were really keen to try. I'm sure that Grandpa found it hard to take a back seat, but he stayed out of it and let the boys get moving. They did a good job, doing a little bit each day when they weren't distracted by tennis and cricket on television.

Then school started, Saturday sport started, and the job stopped. Grandpa got stuck into the job, finished the first tree, finished the second tree, and then, while we weren't looking, took out the third, smaller, tree which we had planned to keep. Being now wiser than I used to be, I bit my tongue and thanked him.

I grew marrows in the space for a year, and the neighbour's apple tree started to put on growth. In two years the apple tree doubled in size and height, and had a huge crop. In autumn, when the apples were ripe, the same parrots that used to feed from the lilly pilly took the apples apart day after day.

Then Grandpa bought two apricot trees and planted them in the space, where they flourished for a while. They are in their third year, he has had several kilograms of very sound apricots from them, and they seem, at a casual glance, like very healthy trees. However, when you look closely, there are ominous signs; some branches are already dying off, because the neighbour who owns the apple tree also owns an apricot tree riddled with gummosis.

Our cat Pompey used the lilly pilly tree to leap up into the unenclosed roof cavity of the cubby-house, where she slept in safety.

In New South Wales there are two localities called Lilli Pilli. One is a suburb on Port Hacking, postcode 2229, facing across the water the northern edge of Royal National Park. The extremity of this tiny peninsula is the attractively named Lilli Pilli Point, and adjacent to this, as if to demonstrate how overuse of alliteration destroys poetry, is Lilli Pilli Point Park. The other Lilli Pilli, postcode 2536, is near Bateman's Bay. The spelling used for the place names is one of several spellings used for the tree.

Yard's End

Listen to the
lilly pilly frolic
of birds in fruit.

If I was thirsty
for flesh and fruit
I'd pluck blue bruise
out of the sky

crush it and crack
without chatter
drop stones as litter
and leave.

Listen to this
lilly pilly frolic
in fruit.

Listen to birds.

Giant of Stuttgart

They were all watching as his arthritic fingers dealt with the ribbons and the wrapping paper.

When he found the packet of bean seeds among his birthday presents, the very old man looked up, smiled, read the name of the variety from the packet, and said he had once spent some months in Stuttgart.

This was news to the family assembled for the party. On the rare occasions when the very old man spoke of his youth, they all paid close attention.

He had been eighteen years old, the war was just over, and he had joined his brother's team of builders to work on a row of shops in the centre of Stuttgart.

These shops (though he had no way of knowing this) were destroyed during a bombing raid in the next war, but the very old man was already in Australia then.

In his old age, he had become a famous grower of back yard beans, and Giant of Stuttgart was a variety he had not met before.

ANNUAL CLIMBING BEANS
LONG PODDED
1062 – GIANT OF STUTTGART
Heaviest yielding, most vigorous and best tasting of all the climbing beans. Stringless beans can be expected over a three-month period. Many customers claim it to be the best bean ever. Provide a 2–3 m trellis. Outstanding. 70c/pkt.

The very old man planted the seeds he had been given in a trench he had prepared with care, along a trellis in a patch of ground alongside the path. The use of this space had been vaguely agreed between the very old man and the younger man in whose house he lived.

During the weeks in which the first planting of Giant of Stuttgart beans grew and grew, the very old man built a second trellis, on the other side of the path, and constructed a number of cross pieces between the two trellises, so that when the beans reached the top of the trellis on the western side of the path they were easily persuaded to extend their reach further. He planted more beans on the other side of the path and eventually that stretch of garden was a green arbour of Giant of Stuttgart beans and looked beautiful from the house.

The younger man agreed with his wife that the beans looked fresh and green, but complained that when he looked closely he could see a trellis made of rusting water pipes with splintered stakes and dried prunings tied to it. The younger man did not like the very old man building structures in his yard but, although he found them ugly and complained to his wife about them, he did not wish to speak to the very old man on the subject.

It was a good year for beans. It was a good year for white fly, too, unless you were the gardener, in which case it was a bad year for white fly.

Then one day in January, when the younger man

arrived home early and went to the vegetable garden to start the water on his cucumbers, he noticed that the beans were glistening with moisture and that the very old man had left a bottle and a spray on a chair by the shed door. The bottle, which the younger man had never seen before, contained a garden spray of great toxicity.

The younger man was trying to run a pesticide-free garden.

The very old man had spent this hot January day in shorts and singlet, working in the shed and garden, and early in the afternoon had sprayed his beans. The younger man was ready to be angry, but when he spoke to the very old man he discovered that he had sprayed the white fly without any protection for himself, standing underneath the beans while he sprayed the growth above the path.

With the spray drifting and settling on bare arms, bare legs, chest, face, bald head. Drifting into eyes and mouth and nose. Breathed in.

The fine print on the label of the pesticide was full of threat. The younger man and his wife read the label to the very old man, louder and louder as he argued that it was all nonsense, and then forced him to take a warm bath and wash himself all over. While he did so, all the clothes he had worn were put through the washing machine; the younger man went back to his garden and his wife began preparing the evening meal.

The younger man in the garden; the wife taking the opportunity to put through more loads of washing; the range hood in the kitchen removing the cooking smells and heat; the very old man in the bath. The door of the very old man's room slightly ajar; his radio playing.

The very old man in his bathroom, and still in the bath one hour, two, two-and-a-half hours later; the bath getting colder and colder; the very old man unable to get out and feeling weak; his voice unheard in a sprawling house with a radio playing, a washing machine working, a range hood running.

Not in his room reading the paper and waiting for his evening meal.

When the very old man was discovered shivering, wrinkled skin in the cold water, voice failed, clutching the side of the bath to prevent himself from slipping down, there was panic, dressing in pyjamas and gown, calling the ambulance, a trip to Casualty.

The younger man took the bottle of garden spray to the hospital and left it with the doctors to help them work out how to treat the very old man.

Next day in the ward the very old man was warm. His voice had returned, and he was being given the honour of his ninety years by nurses younger than his grand-daughters, and he was covered in a red and mottled blotch that had flowered overnight on arms, legs, chest and back.

214

And the medical students were brought in to try their hand at checking him out, and to look at an allergic reaction neither they nor the doctors had seen before.

And the very old man's arms and legs and chest and back were photographed as a record.

And the younger man called the very old man a 'silly old bugger' to everyone except the very old man himself.

And the very old man wondered why they had left him in the bath so long, and whether it showed how much they cared for him; and decided for himself that the spraying and the rash were coincidental, not cause and effect.

And the younger man and his wife worried that the very old man would think they had forgotten him, and wondered if he was feeling upset and angry with them, and if he believed they had ignored him deliberately, and decided they had made a mistake years before in not making clear their rules about sharing a garden.

And knew that they couldn't do so now, without great hurt.

And knew that there would be beans again next year.

Wakefield Press has been publishing good Australian books for over fifty years. For a catalogue of current and forthcoming titles, or to add your name to our mailing list, send your name and address to

Wakefield Press,
Box 2266, Kent Town, South Australia 5071.

TELEPHONE (08) 362 8800   FAX (08) 362 7592

Wakefield Press thanks Wirra Wirra Vineyards
and Arts SA for their support.